# WAY *of*
# Shamanism

# *In the same series:*

Thorsons WAY *of* **Chakras**
*Caroline Shola Arewa*

Thorsons WAY *of* **Crystal Healing**
*Ronald Bonewitz, PhD*

Thorsons WAY *of* **Meditation**
*Christina Feldman*

Thorsons WAY *of* **Native American Traditions**
*Arthur Versluis*

Thorsons WAY *of* **Natural Magic**
*Nigel Pennick*

Thorsons WAY *of* **Psychic Protection**
*Judy Hall*

Thorsons WAY *of* **Reiki**
*Kajsa Krishni Börang*

Thorsons WAY *of* **Reincarnation**
*Judy Hall*

Thorsons WAY *of* **Tarot**
*Evelyne Herbin and Terry Donaldson*

Thorsons WAY *of* **Tibetan Buddhism**
*Lama Jampa Thaye*

Thorsons WAY *of* **Wicca**
*Vivianne Crowley*

Thorsons WAY *of* **Zen**
*Martine Batchelor*

# WAY *of*
# Shamanism

## Leo Rutherford

Thorsons

Thorsons
An Imprint of HarperCollins*Publishers*
77–85 Fulham Palace Road
Hammersmith, London W6 8JB

The Thorsons website address is: www.thorsons.com

and *Thorsons*
are trademarks of
HarperCollins Publishers Limited

First published as *Principles of Shamanism* by Thorsons 1996
This new edition published by Thorsons 2001

3 5 7 9 10 8 6 4 2

© Leo Rutherford 1996

Leo Rutherford asserts the moral right
to be identified as the author of this work

A catalogue record for this book
is available from the British Library

ISBN 0 00 712004 4

Printed and bound in Great Britain by
Martins the Printers Limited, Berwick upon Tweed

# Contents

# Acknowledgements

With thanks to all my many teachers along the road, especially Joan Halifax who got me into all this; Gabrielle Roth who showed me I had body and it needed to dance; Harley Swiftdeer who got me wheeling and seeing in circles; Prem Das who showed me simplicity; Will Shultz and Marilyn Kriegel who pushed me through three very fruitful and quite hard years from which I ended up with a degree; Bob Hoffman and the Quadrinity crew who helped me erase a chunk of my parental history; don Eduardo Calderon and Alberto Villoldo who took me on a journey that changed something inside me forever; and The Wolf whose particular magic I met only recently.

Enormous thanks also to all those who have come to my workshops over the last eighteen years and trusted me enough to enable me to perform the role of guide, especially to all the Magpies, and to all the wonderful Eagle's Wing extended family. Thanks also to all who contributed to the personal experiences quoted in this book, including my friend and colleague Howard Charing, and my friend Kenneth Meadows who blazed a trail.

And to all those indigenous people who have opened their ancient knowledge to help us 'civilized' folks to heal ourselves before, perhaps, we cause so much damage to our Planet that no one lives here any more.

# Introduction

I began what I call my 'second life' at the age of forty. I was a walking wreck – exhausted, burnt out, depressed, irritable and generally miserable to be with – and I couldn't get away from me! I had been running a factory for twelve years, with modest success; however after ten years my physical and mental health had begun to suffer.

There was a definite moment of nemesis when I knew my path must change. One Saturday morning in 1973 I was standing in the centre of the factory and about 20 feet away from me, for no apparent reason, the roof began to collapse. I stood spellbound as one bay after another came down in a hail of dust and thundering noise. A whole portion of the building, about 3,500 square feet, became rubble in moments. Under this area people were working – a moment before it had been a thriving department of rotary tinplate cutting machines. By some miracle no one was injured, never mind killed.

It was later discovered that someone had driven a fork-lift truck into a roof stanchion which had collapsed. That brought down the roof of one bay and other bays followed, domino-like. It felt to me as if the roof had fallen in on my life. At that moment a decision I had been avoiding was made: my life must change radically.

At this time I was managing director of the company, and for ten years I had directed all my energy and skills into it. But in many ways it would be truer to say that I had run it for about eight years and for the last two it had run me. I was physically, emotionally and mentally exhausted. I was living a life which simply did not satisfy my cravings for a deeper sense of purpose, a deeper level of intimacy with people in general, and a love life that made at least a pretence of working.

From that moment it took two more years to get the business back in good order, ready to be taken over by another company. Finally I was able to take my life apart and start again. This came at a time when alternative psychotherapies were coming onto the British scene, mainly from California, and something inside me said this was the way to go. I went to a few therapy weekends at Quaesitor, a personal growth centre in London and discovered that I didn't know the difference between a thought and a feeling. I had learnt to be so defensive that the idea of answering someone truthfully if asked how I felt was quite beyond me. I realized I had a long journey ahead of me.

I had been born at the end of the depression to a family who had lost their first-born child a year earlier. I was cared for by nannies for my first three years because in her deep distress my mother couldn't cope, and my father couldn't look at me because I reminded him of my dead sister. Slowly I grew up with a double message. It felt as if the Universe wanted me and didn't want me at the same time, or at least it didn't want me the way I was, only if I wasn't myself. I tried to become a person who fitted in, who was wanted. I was sent to the 'best schools' – preparatory followed by public school – but I felt an outcast. The best I could do was to achieve a high level of mediocrity, except for a period when I was around 12 or 13 years old when I became Captain of Model Trains (yes really), won a cup for woodwork, and made all sorts of creative things with Meccano. I pretty well failed at all the things which were supposed to be the most important, like football and cricket but succeeded modestly, when I could be bothered, at academic exams. However through all that time a deep feeling stayed with me that the world was not really the way I was told it was and that my problems and limitations were not actually all my fault. I felt I was in the wrong family and being put through the wrong education in order to live in a wrong-way world to satisfy upside-down people who all believed in a judgmental and vindictive god! I look back now having, in a sense, lived two adult lives – 20 years in (straight) industry and 20 years in the Alternative Movement – and I see just how right that feeling was and how it kept me from being completely 'educated' out of myself.

Twenty years ago I felt as if I was all used up. I had put all my energy into my job and left my emotional life to dry up. How many millions of Westerners do that? I reached my low point in 1976 when I felt so bad that at Christmas I decided, 'Well, I'll get some pleasure out of life if it kills me!' So I ate and ate and ate again at my sister's wonderful Christmas dinner. Fortunately no one else noticed my greed, but I had stomach pains for a month afterwards. It was a visit to the Findhorn Foundation in Scotland that lifted my spirits and left me feeling that all was not lost. And quite accidentally, it pointed me in the direction of California and the magic, crazy city of San Francisco.

It was the summer of 1977 when I arrived in San Francisco and it 'said' to me 'All you need to heal yourself is here'. So on my return to England I rented out my cottage and off I went. I became a 'workshop junkie'. I participated in many diverse workshops, including 'God, Sex And Your Body' with Gabrielle Roth; metal bending; mime for beginners; theatre improvisation; psychic awareness training;

and the heavy duty three-month-long Fischer-Hoffman Quadrinity process. The latter was a deep working-through of parental issues to heal the inner child. Mine was in great distress and had been for years, though I did not realize the full extent of it till then.

In order to stay in San Francisco I needed to have a visa. To do that I became an 'official' student and I found a University degree course which was just the kind of programme I would have created for myself: the Holistic Psychology MA at Antioch University, a fully accredited Liberal Arts College. This started with a term which included encounter group, meditation, Feldenkrais body movement, 'inner' sports (sports played with inner awareness as well as outer action) and many lectures and discussions. It was effectively an 11-week workshop – the brainchild of Will Schutz who brought the theory and practice of Humanistic and Transpersonal Psychology into a University setting.

At the beginning of the second year Joan Halifax came to give a course on Cross-Cultural Anthropology. This was my introduction to shamanism, the teachings of the ancients and especially the North American Indians. It was as if a door into a wisdom had opened for me from a place I had never thought to look. The more I studied the more I found it touched me and the more I felt it spoke to the *me-that-I-am*, without telling me, as other spiritual ways I had dallied with seemed to, that I was not right as I am, and that in order to be 'spiritual' I would have to make myself fundamentally different. The medicine wheel put things into perspective for me, showing me the relationships between psychology, psychotherapy, psychic abilities and spirituality and how they are all part of one journey.

Around this time I went on my first wilderness trip – two weeks in the Sierra mountains backpacking, something I'd never done before. I had met Steven Foster and Meredith Little, who led the movement to bring the vision quest to people of all races. But I thought that the three-day and night solo quest which they were offering was too much for me to bite off for a first time. Instead I signed up for a two-week trip with Robert Greenway and Steve Harper through the Esalen Institute. I thought it would be an easier deal, but I was wrong about that. Not only did the trip include a vision quest, it also included a peyote ceremony, a sweat lodge and a three-day hike over Bishop Pass at 11,000 feet into the Kings Canyon National park (three days to hike in means three days to hike out!). At the tender age of 44 I was the oldest inexperienced backpacker by a long way. It was quite a tough trip, even for the hardy ones. I didn't sleep for the first three nights, so when the time came for us to find wilderness names, mine was easy. I became 'Stargazer' because that's what I did all night! Eventually I just got used to sleeping on the hard ground. I tell more of this story in Chapter Seven.

Just after the workshop with Joan Halifax, another teacher of shamanism, Prem Das, came to the University's undergraduate programme. Graduate students were able to take undergraduate courses free if there was space, so I signed up. Prem Das (Paul Adams) had served a long apprenticeship with don Jose Matsewa, the famed 100-year-old Huichol shaman from Mexico, and he taught in their tradition which included chanting and drumming and the use of the cactus peyote to achieve altered states. His course concluded with an all-night peyote ceremony in Huichol traditional style. This took place on the slopes of Mount Tamalpias, just north of San Francisco. My journey to re-vision my world had started. I felt as if I was moving beyond 'rational man', that I was reconnecting with something I had known in the early part of my life before the outer world had taken me over. I felt life was beginning to make some sense again, that I was recovering parts of my soul, and that, at last, I was walking a path to somewhere good.

## ONE

# WHAT IS
# Shamanism?

Shamanism is the oldest way in which humanity has sought connection with Creation. The origins of shamanism go back at least 40,000 – 50,000 years to Stone Age times. All of us have evolved from shamanic cultures – shamanism is not imported, it is our roots wherever we live.

Anthropologists have studied shamanism in North, Central and South America, Africa, amongst the aboriginal people of Australasia, the Eskimo and Lapps of the far north, in Indonesia, Malaysia, Senegal, Patagonia, Siberia, Bali, Ancient Britain and across Europe, in Tibet where the path of Bon shamanism underlies Tibetan Buddhism – in places all over the world. I myself have learned from Inca and Shipibo of Peru, Lakota, Cherokee, Pueblo, Hopi and Ojibway of North America, and from apprentices of the Huichols of Mexico. All over the world there is evidence of shamanic practices from as far back as the Palaeolithic period. From ancient cave drawings and similar records it seems that all indigenous peoples shared a similar cosmology, a similar understanding of how the Universe works. Today shamanism survives on all inhabited continents in less 'developed' regions in spite of the relentless onslaught of Western scientific materialism, the treatment of the Earth and nature as something to be dominated and exploited, and dogmatic male-dominated religion. Now, as the unsustainable nature of Western civilization is becoming visible, more and more people of the industrial world are turning to the old cultures for help and guidance in finding a way back to a greater balance with nature, with Planet Earth, and with themselves.

# *Who or What is a Shaman?*

The word *shaman* comes from the language of the Tungus reindeer herders of the Lake Baikal region of Russia. From the Encyclopaedia Britannica it seems it is derived from the Tunguso-Manchurian word *saman*, formed from the verb *sa,* meaning 'to know', as in the French word *savoir* and the Spanish *saber*. Western anthropologists researching indigenous healing practices the world over have applied the term *shaman* to indigenous healers, visionaries, seers, prophets and their ways. Hence what we know today as shamanism. The anthropologist S. Shirokogoroff, who was one of the earliest to explore the Tungus people, stated:

> *In all Tungus languages this term (saman) refers*
> *to persons of both sexes who have mastered*
> *spirits, who at their will can introduce these*
> *spirits into themselves and use their power over*
> *the spirits in their own interests, particularly*
> *helping other people who suffer from the spirits.*
>
> S. SHIROKOGOROFF *PSYCHOMENTAL COMPLEX OF THE TUNGUS,*
> LONDON, ROUTLEDGE, KEGAN, PAUL, 1935

The words *witch* and *wizard* come from the Indo-European root meaning 'to see' or 'to know', as found in the French *voir* or the Latin *videre* meaning to see, or the German *wissen* meaning to know. In the history of Britain, witchcraft, wicca and wyrd were all shamanic ways. Witchcraft in particular has had many centuries of bad press and the word witch has come to mean something very different from 'to know', 'wise one' or 'wise woman'. Wyrd has been changed into weird – strange. All this was part of the destruction of the ancient spiritual ways wrought by Christianity to facilitate its imposition.

3

Power, knowledge, vision and prophetic abilities are in themselves beyond morality. A shaman is someone who uses these abilities for healing and wholeness (holyness). Someone who uses these same abilities for gain at the expense of others, for evil, is often called a sorcerer (although the original meaning of that word is simply 'one who connects with the source'). Witchcraft was originally a 'white' path of healing but became corrupted by some and is remembered in the cultural folklore mainly as 'dark'. It is important to remember at all times that power is just power, an ability is just an ability. It is what we humans do with these that makes them good or evil.

The meaning of shaman is sometimes quoted as 'to heat up, to burn, to work with heat and fire' and sometimes as 'Wise One' or 'One Who Knows', 'One Who Sees'. In the words of Mercia Eliade, a shaman is a *Master of Ecstasy* – a master of *ex-stasis* (from the Greek), meaning outside the normal stasis of consciousness. They are masters of altered states of consciousness in which the normal rules of Newtonian three-dimensional existence are no longer valid, and in which travel to other worlds, precognition, distant seeing and healing, communication with the dead, are all possible and natural.

'Ordinary' people, in the words of the Armenian teacher Gurdjieff, live in a state of 'waking sleep'. The shaman is someone who has woken up to true reality, the reality of the 'nagual', the reality behind apparent reality, the reality of imagination. The common-place statement 'Oh, it's only imagination' is a gross denial of not only the whole realm of the magical but of any understanding of how the universe really works. This is where the shaman works: in the realm of cause, in the imagination, the thought or dream realm where all is conceived and of which this familiar third dimension of gross material reality is but a reflection.

Consider, for example, the room or building you are sitting in, or a building nearby. What came first, 'reality' or the thought? Surely the thought! Someone thought of the building, imagined it, or we could say 'dreamed' it. Then architects came to convert the vision, the idea, into plans, and then came the quantity surveyor to estimate the materials required. Only lastly did the builders enter to create 'reality', the building itself!

# Definitions of Shamanism

*Shamanism is not a belief system.* It is a path to knowledge which is gained through experience of many facets of life, through rituals, ceremonies, prayer and meditation, trials and tests. Knowledge is something that works, that stands up to tests and to the test of time, that is known from inside, unlike belief which is something taken on from outside, from others. Wars are fought over beliefs, dogma and doctrine, never over knowledge.

There are some different ideas amongst Western students of shamanism as to exactly what shamanism is and isn't. It seems that the Tungus shamans, in common with many other tribes and peoples, used the shamanic journey with the steady monotonous beat of the drum (*see Chapter Six*) as their primary method of travelling to the spirit world and finding what they needed for healing. Dr Michael Harner, the American anthropologist, has popularized this method for Westerners and spread much good knowledge. I had the pleasure of studying with him back in 1981 and '82 at his workshops. He calls this process 'core shamanism'. Unfortunately this is sometimes taken to mean that it is the *only* core of shamanism, which it most certainly is not. If we understand the meaning of the word 'shamanism' to be the ancient healing practices of indigenous

5

peoples worldwide, then there are many other methods than journeying, though the one thing they all have in common is communication and interaction with the spirit world. For example, in the Minianka tribe in Mali, the shaman is the drummer whose task it is to drum the people, in their nightly dances, into a state of balance and harmony. *The Healing Drum* by Yaya Diallo describes these rituals.

A cross-cultural survey of 42 indigenous shamanic cultures by Peters and Price-Williams, published in 1980, found 18 where the shamans worked with spirit possession only, 10 where they worked with magical flight only, 11 with both and three in which neither concept was used to explain the trance state. (L. Peters, ed. Shirley Nicholson, *Shamanism*, Quest Books). As you can see there is plenty of variety. For example, is a medium a shaman? With these definitions it depends just how she works. Does she go into a trance and become possessed or does she go on a flight? We get into a real Western rational reductionist shambles trying to sort this out. A much better approach is that of Roger N. Walsh from *The Spirit of Shamanism*:

> *Shamanism can be defined as a family of*
> *traditions whose practitioners focus on*
> *voluntarily entering altered states of*
> *consciousness in which they experience*
> *themselves or their spirit(s), travelling to other*
> *realms at will, and interacting with other entities*
> *in order to serve their community.*

My preference is to take the term as a broad umbrella covering ancient indigenous holistic healing practices worldwide. The overall way of defining shamanism that most satisfies me is inclusive and holistic and can be understood through the description of the classic journey from apprentice to shaman described by the medicine wheel teachings of the Native Americans (*See Chapter Three*). The first step is 'erasing personal history' which means healing those aspects of one's past which interfere with life in the present. The second step is 'facing your death and making death your ally' – facing the mortality of this life in the eternity of existence, separating from one's culture and its mores and opening to the Spirit and Sacred Law. The third step is 'stopping the world' – clearing the mind of its inner dialogue and mental garbage, replacing beliefs taken on from outside with knowledge and wisdom from the deep well within. The fourth is 'controlling the dream and finding new vision and purpose' – rebirth as a renewed person with new reasons for being. The final step is to the centre of one's circle and the taking of full responsibility for one's existence as an Impeccable Warrior of the Spirit. This is the path of the warrior. A shaman, then, is someone who has fully walked this path of transformation and chosen to become a healer, helper, seer, prophet, in service to the people. This is a map of the journey we all take if we wish to grow into the fullness of ourselves. Many mythologies describe the great journey in different ways, but the basic steps are the same.

## Shamanism and Sickness

In tribal cultures, the shaman is the 'doctor of the soul' for both the community and for individuals. He or she is concerned with the health – the spirit – of the community and with keeping alive the vision of who they are and where they are going. The shaman's primary task is to keep the people as a whole 'in spirit' – inspired – and secondarily to assist any individual who suffers from loss of spirit/soul – who becomes, in modern day language, dispirited.

WAY of

The shamanic understanding of sickness is of a loss of power. Power here refers to energy, not might. It is power over oneself, being power full. When we are full of power we are unlikely to get sick and from a classical shamanic point of view, bad spirits, intrusions, or darts sent from another person will not succeed in harming us. From a Western point of view this is the same as saying that we are vulnerable to sickness when we feel bad, when life is emotionally difficult and we are in a state of grief or (repressed) rage. Prior to the time I changed my life, when I was basically discontented and subject to depression, I would get every cold and flu that came around. Since I got my life in good order I am hardly ever sick. (Although I feel I am tempting fate by stating this!)

Shamans say the main cause of illness is 'separation', meaning separation from nature, from community, from the Source, from Oneness. Interestingly, the original meaning of 'sin' is to be separated from god, to 'miss the mark'.

From a shamanic point of view, unaware, 'separated' people cause damage when their hostility, bad vibes and dark thoughts penetrate others. We send out thought forms all the time. When we send good thoughts, they can bless, and when we send bad thoughts they can harm. In the great web of life all things influence all things. Shamanic work is about contacting the powers of the universe directly, about ending separation from nature, from the source, and therefore we can say it is about healing 'sin'!

## Perennial Philosophy

In the Perennial Philosophy it is said there are two distinct paths to enlightenment, the 'Via Positiva' or path of involvement in the world and the senses, and the 'Via Negativa' or path of renunciation. The latter includes Yoga, monastery life – the path of the nun and the monk, the way of the sannyasin (except Rajneesh who reversed its meaning), the aesthetic way, denial of the body, the senses, sexuality, the flesh, the Earth. It is the path of getting off the wheel of life entirely, and is an age-old respected path. When it degenerates, however, it becomes puritanical and negating, it sees the earth as evil, and the sole purpose of life can become to 'sit on the right hand of god in paradise'. From this point of view, the Earth and its pollution simply don't matter so long as 'I' can get to heaven. Extremists of this path are potentially a danger to the rest of us who want to continue to live on the Earth.

The 'Via Positiva' is the shamanic way, the tantric way, the way of full involvement in life, in the Earth, in the senses, in dance, in sexuality as a path to the transcendent. Enlightenment comes through the senses, through learning to work with many states of consciousness, through working with all the many senses of the body – not just the 'official' five. The Earth is our home and we are part of her, not separate. Heaven is here and now and so is hell, according to how we make our experience of reality. We are Spirit Beings placed here on Earth to learn. Mother Earth is our school where we come to evolve, which it seems we cannot do as well in the other dimensions of existence. We are supposed to look after our Great Mother and nurture her, not destroy her with ignorant, acquisitive greed and sensual debauchery, which is the degenerate side of this path. The Via Positiva celebrates life and all its lessons, the body as the human Temple Of Experience, the body of the Earth as Sacred and Divine. This book is about the Via Positiva.

# A Shaman's View of Western Culture

Looking at our culture and history from a shamanic point of view, it seems we in this Western rational, technological, Christian culture have picked up some extraordinary ideas. It is as if we have become blinded by the apparent reality, what's 'out there', and have forgotten the importance of what is 'in here' – that we have lost a sense of the intimate connection between the two. We have even created a 'god' that is half a god, all masculine and no feminine. We have split 'good' from 'evil' as if one can cut a coin in half, and we have placed our object of worship somewhere out in the sky and most certainly not anywhere near the Earth. We have condemned ourselves and our children as 'miserable sinners', judged wrong and bad, steeped in 'original sin' even as we are born! We have developed an elevated idea of ourselves as the superior beings on the planet with the right to use, exploit, 'develop' whatever we wish, and have even persuaded our 'god' to support us in this fantasy. It is as if we have lost our inner life and overdeveloped the outer in an attempt to make up for the loss. Surely we will be looked back upon by our descendants as very peculiar ancestors!

Very many people in the Western world have been spiritually disenfranchised. We have had centuries of dogma, of having to give power away to the churches and their priests who claimed 'god' for their own and came between the people and the Creator, leaving many people believing that they had no such direct connection. The people were also medically disenfranchised when the female midwives, herbalists, healers and helpers of the community were dubbed as witches and murdered, burnt at the stake. That is largely how the medical profession came to be a male preserve. The people were taught that they must put their faith in the doctor and not in their own inner knowing or healing power. All this meant a tremendous loss of individual responsibility and personal feelings of self-worth. A human was then seen like a vehicle which had to be taught how to behave, told what to think and believe and put right if it broke down! So we became disconnected to the earth and to ourselves, pitted against our natural instincts and lost in the world of outer effect, valuing ourselves mainly by our individual achievements.

We are collectively suffering from enormous soul loss. This is evidenced by so much feeling of meaninglessness, by self-hatred and abuse through drink, drugs, pornography, rape, child abuse, theft, lack of respect for the earth. These are the dis-eases of our time, of our society, which will kill us unless fruitful change takes place. These dis-eases make a war within the self. War within the self easily becomes war with another, and then war between groups, then between countries. War begins inside like everything else, and if not healed it spreads like a cancer till we have a warlike, competitive society.

In the context of the failure of the Western 'dream' of a life of riches and ease to bring lasting happiness and fulfilment, the rebirth of interest in shamanism and the wisdom of the Ancients is timely. If we are to survive the human desecration of our Mother Planet we need all the help we can get. We are collectively like a paranoid being, terrified of parts of ourselves. Last year worldwide we spent approximately one trillion dollars on weapons for defence. It is reckoned that it would require a mere 12 billion dollars to end global starvation and yet we spend over 80 times as much defending ourselves from each other. We have holes in the ozone layer, yet the number of cars on the road steadily increases, as does the number of jets flying the air routes. The rain forests are cut down; last year the size of a large US state such as Oklahoma is reckoned to have gone. But the rain forests are the planet's lungs, the oxygen producers of the earth and what will happen if we start running short of oxygen?

There is something very strange in the way we do our collective accounts. The former World Bank economist Herman Daly has said that the current national accounting systems of developed countries treat the Earth as a business in liquidation. For example, pollution shows up three times in the Gross Domestic Product account as a gain: once when the factory produces it as a by-product of some-thing useful, secondly when the nation spends billions cleaning up the mess and thirdly in the extra costs of health care and environ-mental recovery! (*Source Resurgence* magazine). So if you feel you are getting poorer even though the papers are telling you the gross wealth is going up every year, that is one explanation.

We live in a take-away society. People are honoured for how much they take away – how rich they become. This is quite opposite to many an indigenous society where people were honoured for how much they gave, how much they contributed. This feeling of need to take comes from a consciousness of scarcity, which is at the root of a competitive society. This mind-set says 'there is not enough and never going to be enough and I must grab my bit before anything runs out.' By comparison, a typical indigenous society has a mind-set which says 'the earth provides, its resources renew each year and that produce must be shared amongst all or the people will die'. A man with two horses naturally gives one to a man with none. A man with no horse in a horse-based society cannot fulfil his role. Imagine someone here with two cars looking around for someone with none and giving one away!

The hazard of nuclear weapons and nuclear power hangs over us like a sword of Damocles. The problems of Chernobyl are not over, it seems, and there are nuclear submarines in heaven knows what sort of condition buried in the sea north of Russia, veritable time bombs waiting to wreak havoc. We currently face a situation without known precedent in the history of humanity.

This is a time of incredible possibilities with the birth of the most amazing communications systems, and a time of the most grave dangers to the very infrastructure of the planet herself. Our triumphs of technology and science have not been accompanied by equivalent advances in spiritual, emotional, and inner moral development, and now we have all we require to wipe ourselves off the face of the planet and take much other life with us. Currently we are collectively like an unhappy, disturbed, depressed individual contemplating suicide – all the pills (or bombs) are lined up ready to be used – and we wonder if it is going to be worthwhile taking all the trouble to sort ourselves out!

Many old cultures have myths which say this has all happened before. That we are the fourth or fifth world, and we are now at that crucial point of time that all the others reached where we must advance spiritually or die. The myths say that up until now each time humanity has failed at this point and had to start over again. Now we must either dream a new dream – of sharing and caretaking, loving and supporting each other, demolishing our defences and feeding the hungry, of mutual co-operation all over the Earth, of ceasing excessive pollution and voluntarily reducing our standard of living to one that is fully sustainable – or face the likelihood of virtual extinction.

There is a great need now to forge our own individual connections with the Source and empower ourselves again. To accept responsibility for our lives, our connection to spirit, our health, our actions in the world, and most importantly our actions regarding our home, Mother Earth. The shamans say we are supposed to be the Caretakers of the Earth. We are the one species with the knowledge of Self, and thus the power of conscious choice. We are now challenged as never before to awaken to our Oneness with All Things, to our relationship to each other as cells in the body of The Creator manifest in and on the Earth, and to use our vast power wisely.

It is time to change our mind-set, dream a new dream and re-mythologize ourselves and our society. The return of the ways and the teachings of the shamans is here to help and guide us in going forward into a way of beauty. The essence of the shamanic way, adapted to the needs of urban, suburban and country people of today, can be a framework, a set of guidelines and tools which can help us in this monumental task. We have learned much in the last thousands of years; it is not simply a case of thinking that modern is bad and ancient is good, but that we can find pieces we have lost along the way by looking backward to reconnect with our roots and with ancient wisdom.

## *The Revival of Shamanistic Ways*

The whole scene of alternative workshops and courses is like a giant spontaneous university which has sprung up in the last 25 – 30 years and which is serving the change in paradigm that is essential if we are to survive on Planet Earth. If we look back we can find the roots of this change in the latter part of the last century: in the Theosophical Society of the 1880s, through the works of Alice

Bailey, Freud, Jung, Reich and others; in the many humanistic and transpersonal therapies; in the coming of Buddhism and Eastern religions to the West: in the sixties revolution, rock'n'roll, the rave scene of the 1990s; and of course in the opening up by the shamans of their ancient wisdom kept in secret for millennia until the time was right. In a broad sense all can be seen as a kind of shamanistic revival. This revival involves connecting directly to the place of knowing without priests or dogma stuck in between, entering the visionary worlds to connect with one's own spirit teachers and bring back one's own guidance and knowledge. It is an attempt by the people to claim back power and rights – the right to our own spirituality, the right to doctor ourselves for our own health, the right to think for ourselves, the right to dance to our own rhythms and to decide how we wish to live and what mores we choose to live by.

The hunger today for spiritual experience, for finding meaning and purpose in life, is enormous. Unfortunately some experience is grasped at with little knowledge or consideration of the possible consequences. I mentioned the rave scene. This is a movement which has the potential to facilitate a change of values and world view for many young people. Or rather it would have if there were elders and shamans to guide and help the young people to discriminate between what is of value and what is chaff. Accessing altered states can be of little use unless you can bring back the visions, ground them and actualize them creatively in the everyday world. Escape gets us nowhere – literally no-where. In the words of the late Chippewa Medicine Man Sun Bear: 'Don't tell me about your visions unless they grow corn.'

I see the 'Alternative University' as the greatest hope for fruitful change in the developed world. It is through re-education that we can find ways to go forward. Guidance is available to assist us to work through and release those pieces of personal history which still hurt, which come between ourselves and our ability to be truly present in the 'now'; one can find help to face deep level changes in the structure of one's life that may be necessary to achieve a really meaningful existence; guidance to find the courage needed to take responsibility for ourselves and cease complaining and blaming others; to find a new, clear vision of why we are alive at this time and what the cosmos wants from us in exchange for this gift of life; to find re-connection with our true and literal mother the Earth, and Father, the Sun.

There was a saying in the sixties: 'Turn on, tune in, drop out.' It didn't work too well because it left out any notion of responsibility. For the nineties, perhaps we can rewrite it: 'Turn on, tune in and take responsibility for yourself, your life and your home – Mother Earth.' We need to work for the benefit of our sister and brother humans and for all kingdoms of our Mother planet. It is not enough just to look after ourselves, we are all part of a community whether we like it or not. Dropping out is no longer a responsible option. It is incumbent on each of us who awakens to work for the good of all and the healing of the Earth.

# TWO

# 'THE WORLD IS AS You Dream It'

*'We do not see things the way they are but as
we are.'*

JEWISH PROVERB.

'The World is as You Dream It' is a quote from Numi, Shuar Shaman
from Ecuador, as reported in John Perkins' book of the same name.
Shamans say that how people live in the everyday world is a product of how they 'see' the world internally; in other words their
mythology – the stories they tell themselves of how things are – represents their 'dream' of themselves and life, and their vision of the
universe and how they fit into it. Growing up in the twentieth century we often experience the universe as hostile and ourselves as
small and powerless, so we tend to give up and try to fit in or else
take it on and try to beat it. Either way, a part of us 'dies' – we
suffer a partial 'soul loss' (*see Chapter 5*).

# *Personal Mythology –*
# *'Dreams I Was Taught'*

I was 'educated' through the British boarding school system, which
was widely regarded as the best education money could buy. I was
sent to board at the age of eight, which gives a strange message to
a child – 'we love you so much we are sending you away'. I found
myself in a frightening environment surrounded by savages! A sort of
penal prison system with punishments for the smallest of transgres-
sions. What had I done to deserve this? I must be dreadfully unlovable
to be discarded and put in this hell. After a couple of crying years I
managed to stem the tears, block my feelings, become a 'normal' boy
– that is, to learn to compete, put others down, rank myself against the
rest and survive... and become a stranger to myself in the process.

At the public school where I suffered for four years from the age of 14 to 18, there was an unwritten but strongly held belief that a boy had no intrinsic value whatever as himself, his worth was only in what he could win – first for the school, second for his house and lastly for himself. One's right to self-esteem and esteem from others was entirely bound up with competitive ability. In the early years you were designated a 'fag' (no sexual connotation in those days) – to fetch and carry at the whim of prefects and seniors in authority. After being thoroughly indoctrinated with the set of beliefs and attitudes of the school (which included the idea that public schoolboys were the elite not just of Britain but of the whole world), in your last year you became a prefect with the power to put the younger boys through the same hell you endured – for their own good, of course. Then when later you become a parent, it can seem natural to put your son through the same agony, as you tend just to remember the final year of power and 'glory' rather than the earlier years of anguish and pain. And so the system perpetuates itself. A real person is broken down and a false competitive, defensive ego, with a hidden terror of its own worthlessness, is created instead. This false ego seems to be so real it feels as if there is no one else inside.

The kind of mores I was taught in childhood and early adolescence went (with perhaps a touch of overstatement) something like this: The world is a scary place and one needs to be careful how one behaves principally because of what other people might think. If you are not like them, and do not hold the 'right' opinions, they might cast you out as unacceptable. Manners are the most important thing in life and sex is something rather nasty to be avoided, at least until one is 'safely married'! Women don't like it and only do it because they love their husbands who, being men, do like it although if they are good religious men, they try not to. Homosexuality is from the devil and one has to be most careful because once seduced into that way of life one is likely to be hooked forever. (No one ever noticed the striking subtext in that!) Marriages are made in heaven by God and last until death regardless of how the couple feels. We must all believe in Jesus, in the resurrection and ascension, do what we are told, think what we are told, believe what we are told, dress as we are told and have a short back and sides haircut (if we are boys) in order to get to heaven and have everlasting life. We ordinary mortals were born in sin and have to be cured from our dreadful natures so we can have our sins forgiven before being worthy of respect in the world. God sits in judgement of us humans and we must love him. Also, the British Empire conquered much of the world for its own good and made lots of primitive countries British and Christian, and weren't they lucky!

This may seem laughable, but I am talking about my experience only fifty or so years ago. Go back another fifty years or a century or so and it was far, far worse, with barbarities such as witch burning, expulsion from the church (which was a virtual death sentence in its time), for heresy if you didn't believe what you were told. What is so important for all of us attempting to awaken from centuries of repression is that these old forced beliefs go very, very deep into the cultural mind. Awakening from the traumas of our individual past is just a small part of awakening from the mind control that has been exercised over the whole culture for centuries. And the forces who kept us in bondage are alive and well and still working hard at it, as can be witnessed in the rise of all sorts of fundamentalism.

# Cultural Mythology – Our Collective 'Dream'

Our collective 'dream', our mythology, has been influenced in Europe for about 2,500 years or more by Aristotelian, and later Cartesian, thought; by the creed of scientific materialism flowing down to us through our root Hindu–Babylonian–Egyptian–Greek–Roman–European–American culture; and for about 1,700 years by organized religion, especially the Roman Catholic Church. The former tells us that reality is just what you see with the physical eyes, hear with the physical ears and touch with the body. There is no subtle energy field around the body or any living thing, no subtle connections or feelings, no spirits, vibes, intuition; the Universe is just a giant machine. To quote Bruce Holbrook from his complex work *The Stone Monkey*:

> *According to the Absolute-Fragmental (ie Western) paradigm, one arbitrarily separates the formless from the formed, the non-absolute from the Absolute, the non-quantifiable from the quantifiable, the non-obvious from the obvious, and then totally ignores the formless-non-absolute-non-quantifiable-non-obvious, handing it over to religious mystics. Or one pretends that it does not exist.*

> BRUCE HOLBROOK, *THE STONE MONKEY*,
> WILLIAM MORROW INC, 1981

Only thus can the 'occult' (which simply means hidden) become something to be feared; what science does not understand becomes the '*super*natural' and natural subtle senses become *extra*-sensory perception. God then becomes either something separate, far away and superhuman, or is simply denied completely. In this view there is no life before birth or after death, in fact there is really no point to it all. But here we are and perhaps the more scientific knowledge we can find, the more we can subjugate the universe and improve our miserable lot! Or have our body cryogenically frozen at death in the hopes of being resuscitated at a later and better time. Just look at what that says about the value of oneself as a human being, and about lack of trust – faith – in the Universe – God.

Religion, on the other hand, gives us a prescription for a sort of static eternal life 'sitting on the right hand of God', but with a giant load of conditions or else we might end up 'burning in the fires of hell'. It seems Christianity, as we know it, was really created at the Council of Nicaea in AD 325 under the direction of the Emperor Constantine, and from the debate of 318 Bishops came the official Nicene Creed. It is the Nicene Creed that transformed the Jewish healer, medium, prophet and teacher (or shaman), Jesus, into 'the (only) son of god, begotten of the father (with no mother) 'for us men and for our salvation'. Not for women, they were not granted souls by the church until much later in 1545. And then only by a majority of three votes! This decision about who Jesus was came 300 years after his death, and was made by people who believed among other such things that the earth was flat. And this decision, hotly argued over at the time, remains the foundation of Christianity today.

We may laugh at the idea that women should be reluctantly granted souls by the male-dominated church, but it should be hollow laughter. Spiritually we have advanced very little indeed. It is only this decade that women have finally been accepted as priests (not priestesses!) in the Church of England. Watching women leave the Church of England to join the Roman Church to reinforce themselves as second class citizens subjected to the dominance of patriarchy shows how powerful indoctrination can be.

Just for a moment let us project ourselves to the centre of the Milky Way, our own galaxy. As we look out upon the myriad galaxies of the Universe, we notice that ours is quite a small one, not special at all. Then we notice that there is organic life on a tiny planet orbiting a small sun on one of the outer wings of our minor galaxy. There is perhaps a touch of arrogance in the self-reflective beings on this planet thinking that the Prime-Creator-Of-All-That-Is is one of them!

There are many religious injunctions against the expression of sexuality. For very strict catholics – no contraception, no masterbation, no sex outside marriage and only sex within marriage if you're trying to procreate! What a recipe for a miserable, 'sinful' existence. What a great way to set a normal human being against their very nature. And isn't that just what has happened – that many of us are set not just against our own natures but against nature herself? To such a horrific extent that we are in danger of exterminating ourselves and much life on this planet.

Let us look again from outer space. Do we not look rather like a race of mad, schizophrenic, psychopathic planet destroyers? Out of touch with our true nature, with the nature of our home, Planet Earth, with the nature of Creation and our relationship to the Creator; with frighteningly low self-regard and self-love; at war with parts of ourselves, especially our sexuality; spending vast resources on armaments 'defending' ourselves against each other? How did we in the West ever get to such a point, dream such an unsustainable dream?

# The Fragmentation of the Western Dream

It seems to me there are three primary splits in the way we have been taught to understand the world. Firstly, we are taught that the Creator God and the Creation are separate instead of one and the same. So let us ask a simple question: If God Creates the Creation what does God Create it out of? It makes no sense whatever until we say that: The Creator Creates The Universe Out Of (It)Self.

Which, of course, has been the shamanic understanding for about 50,000 years! And it is the teaching of Jesus too. In the Peshitta version Syriac Aramaic text of the Gospels, thought to be the earliest known text (probably from the second century AD which was long before 'Christianity' was recognized) the first line of the Lords Prayer is *Abwoon d'bwashmaya*. This is a brief translation:

> A: The Absolute Force, Source, Oneness.
> bw: Birthing, creation, a flow of blessing from the Oneness.
> oo: the Breath or Spirit that carries the flow.
> n: the vibration that becomes form.

There is a fuller translation in *Prayers of the Cosmos* by Neil Douglas-Klotz (Harper Collins). To translate this as 'Our father which art in heaven' meaning a father-god is out there somewhere in the sky controlling everything, is not an accurate translation of a great teaching. However, if we translate father to spiritual mother-father, and heaven to its original Aramaic meaning – the universe – we can also see something closer to the meaning Jesus intended. Hence the first line could be said like this: 'Our Mother-Father-Creator which art (in) the Universe'.

What then is our relationship to the Creator? The Creator is Everything Everywhere, therefore we live *inside* the Creator! We are *all* the 'sons and daughters of God'.

The second split is the idea that *good* and *evil* are separate, and that there is a Devil or Satan lurking to upset God's will. The classic myth of the hero or heroine's journey describes the journey of all of us in life. To be a hero or heroine we need challenges and worthy adversaries. Where would Parsifal be without all the obstacles in his path on the way to find the Holy Grail? Where would Luke Skywalker be without Darth Vader? Where would James Bond be without Smersh? Where is the goodie without the baddie? Where is light without dark?

One thing we often overlook is that we are blinded in the light as well as in the dark. Have you ever been on a ski slope in a snowstorm, when all around you is white, upon a background of white? The sky disappears, the ground disappears, the horizon is no longer there. All you see is white everywhere, all around. In such circumstances it is more than difficult just to stand up, never mind ski anywhere. Or imagine a great painter painting a beautiful picture in pure white upon a white background! Without contrast, we are blinded. Only in the balance of dark and light can we see.

How can a coin have only one face? How can there be a 'god' without a 'devil'? Devil spells 'lived' backwards, evil is 'live' backwards. The word God spells good with just one o difference. Perhaps the words are some of the problem. When we scorn a 'devil' and pray to a 'go(o)d', we are acting as if these are forces outside 'doing something' to us; we are placing ourselves firmly in the role of victim of existence. Once we acknowledge that The Creator is *All Things*, that while our ultimate true nature is evolving and is good, we have a shadow, a tendency to involution, and that the enemy we

*25*

are really fighting is inside – our addictions, fears, laziness, attach-ments, judgements, envy, avarice, self-importance and so on – then we can feel ourselves as being on a journey of evolution. We are expected to choose our path and to be willing to accept responsibil-ity for our self and our actions, and we reap the rewards or otherwise in the universe's great feedback system, karma.

Good and evil can be seen as the forces of evolution and involution. In evolution the ego – sense of self – evolves into deeper and more subtle expressions of itself while remembering it is just a part of The One. In involution the ego, lost in its sense of individuality, forgets it is just a part of the ocean of The One, and in fear of death sets itself up against all that is 'other' in order, it thinks, to save itself. We can express the issue of good and evil as the battle of *good* versus *(involuted) ego!*

In the shamanic tradition, the Creator is understood as All-That-Is. The Native American ultimate term for the Creator is *Great Mystery*, accepting that the force of creation is beyond our capability of knowing. There is no differentiation between the Creator and the Creation – which is seen as the Creator-In-Expression, or *Wakantanka*. There is no Satan or devil, the nearest is Coyote the Trickster. Coyote does not intend evil but is egoic – ignorant, foolish and scheming. But his schemes come back on him in the end as do ours upon us. This mythology is similar to the original understanding of Lucifer, the Light Bringer. Lucifer brings the light through the darkness. We learn through our mistakes. As Spirits living in a body, we each have to struggle with the enemy within. We have to fight our addictions, our ignorance, our laziness, and so on and on. Jesus spends '40 days and nights' in the 'wilderness' of himself. He goes on a vision quest to find his path and he confronts his demonic side, his Satan, his enemy within. Once we truly confront an inner 'demon', wrestle with it and defeat it, it becomes our ally. In psychotherapy circles there is a truism: 'Your clients come to you with your own problems!' This happens because if you have had the problem, wrestled with it and defeated it, you are the ideal person to assist another with a similar problem. You know the landscape from personal experience, not from book learning. You know how to guide a person through this part of the underworld because you have been there.

# The Imbalance of Feminine and Masculine

One more split that matters a great deal is that between the feminine and the masculine. The feminine is defined in many ways: receptive, creative, yin, nurturing, dark, inner, chaotic, Dionysian, the underworld, the place we go to create, the place of mystery and the unknown. The masculine is defined as active, conceptual, yang, light, outer, ordered, Appollonian, the upper world, the place we go to get things done, the place of the known. On the Medicine Wheel these are the west and the east. In our western culture, for many hundred, perhaps thousands of years, these forces have been seriously out of balance. The masculine, the Father, is revered and holds the power. The feminine, the Mother, is feared, ridiculed and disempowered; in extreme cases, burnt at the stake. Women burnt at the stake – Mother Earth's lungs, the forests, slashed and burnt – is there not an uncomfortable analogy here?

It is time to worship the Great Mother again in ceremony, in Church and out on the land. To make this change – to worship again the Holy Spirit, God the Father and God the Mother, a Trinity in balance – will help us change our 'dream', it will remind us that we need to honour Mother Earth as well as Sky Father, woman and the feminine equally with man, to honour those who rear the children who are the future. The first two Great Sacred Laws of the Universe as understood by the Native American people are: *'All is born of woman'* and *'Nothing must be done which will harm the children'.* A return to balance of the images we worship will help us step off the path towards potential self-extinction.

# The Way the Shamanic Cultures Saw Creation

The Creator creates the Creation continuously out of Him/Her/itself, and All-That-Is, the external world, is the Creator-Made-Manifest. As parts of timeless eternity, of the Creation, we existed 'before' human birth and we continue to exist 'after' death, as do all things, though not in the same form or with the same degree of individuality. When we are born in the manifest world we 'die' to the spirit world; when we die to the manifest world we are reborn in the spirit world. From the Bhagavad-Gita:

> *There was never a time when I did not exist, nor*
> *you. Nor is there any future in which we shall*
> *cease to be.*

We are each an individual consciousness on a journey of learning through life. We are not superior or inferior to the animals, plants, minerals, or the planet itself. Our existence is dependent on the planet, the plants, insects, fish, birds, animals – all that came into being before us – and we are part of planet earth and of the sun.

Good and evil are points of view, two sides of the same coin. They are not absolutes, just as in Chinese philosophy the yin is never completely yin and the yang never completely yang. Without the villain, the challenger or hero or heroine has no opportunity to find heroism and grow in wisdom, knowledge and love. Life is intended to be a series of challenges, of moral choices through which we are tested, and we experience the results of our choices through the medium of karma.

We each of us create our own experience of 'reality'. In the words of Casteneda's don Juan, we do not see the world, we only see a description of it according to how we have been taught to see by all the years of cultural conditioning. In magic moments of awakening produced by spiritual practice, ceremony, ecstatic experience or perhaps extreme stress, where we 'stop the world' for a moment, we experience true reality, but the rest of the time we are seeing mainly a reflection of our own projections.

Our internal dialogue is the way we tell ourselves what 'reality' is. We accustom ourselves to substitute thoughts in place of reality. We look out at people, places, objects, ourselves, and at the same time we think about what we are seeing – and then we take our thoughts and feelings for the real thing! And the universe is very obliging. You get up in the morning feeling good, think 'Today will be a good day', your confidence rises with positive feelings, you go out and people respond to your mood and welcome you and reflect your good feelings back onto you so your confidence rises further; women (or men, as appropriate) smile at you and you feel wanted and interesting and worthwhile. Another day dawns and you get out of the famous 'wrong side of bed'. Right away the universe obligingly arranges for things to keep on going wrong. You miss your train by a moment, you spill your coffee, you are bad tempered and grouchy, the person at the newspaper stand serves everyone else when you try to buy a paper, a woman or man snubs you and makes you feel ugly and worthless... and so that day goes on! *'As you believe, so shall it be.'* The outer reflects the inner.

The placebo effect is a well documented phenomenon. I would like to take that a stage further and suggest that the whole of life works rather like a placebo phenomenon. Self-fulfilling prophecies fulfil themselves. Believe something strongly enough and it will tend to happen. A Navaho medicine man makes this point succinctly: 'If the patient really has confidence in me, then he gets cured. If he has no confidence, then that is his problem.' (D.Sandner, *Navaho Symbols of Healing*, Harcourt Brace).

We are like magnets calling events towards us according to our inner beliefs and 'dreams'. Dream it with strongly focused intent, as shamans do, and the universe will respond. Your dream will manifest, though with a time lag during which one must hold fast to the intent. Until we face our learned patterns of thinking, move past the dominance of the habitual internal (un)conscious dialogue, we keep on recreating our life similarly to the way it has been, even though we might change the players and the places. How many people have repetitive relationships which start off with great hopes and descend gradually into the same morass as the one before – inevitably replaying some childhood pattern which has not been brought to consciousness and worked through?

However I would like to inject a word of caution. 'We create our own reality' has become a New Age cliché and there is a problem with taking this statement simplistically. If you are standing in the middle of an earthquake and you say to yourself 'How did *I* create this earthquake?' you are probably undergoing massive ego inflation and giant delusions of grandeur! Do you really imagine that you alone can create a quake? What about all the other humans affected and the animals, birds, plants, insects, rocks? There are an awful lot more of them than you and they all have their agendas too. Such an idea is too preposterous to seriously contemplate and is even dangerous when applied ignorantly in circumstances as, for example, assault or rape. 'How did you create your rape?' is hardly a therapeutic way to help someone. However, if you ask the question 'How did I let myself get into this situation where this bastard raped me?' or 'How did I come to be here in the middle of this earthquake when it happened?' then you are on solid ground(!) with something useful to work with. Did you miss some indications that there was danger? Did you ignore or space out when Spirit gave you a nudge? Have you been walking asleep, preoccupied with 'busy-ness'?

We create – interpret – our own experience of reality, but to think one creates all reality is ignoring the fact that we share the physical planet earth together, and planet earth, her winds, waters, mountains and sometimes fires, will mock the human who dares to think he alone creates it all.

## New Mythos

We humans of the so-called developed world desperately need a new dream. We need to re-mythologize ourselves and our world. We need to balance the great powers of feminine and masculine. We need to cooperate as successfully as we compete. We need to become aware of the finiteness of the earth's resources and to care-take and replenish as we use. We need to share the earth's resources instead of having a winner-takes-all attitude. We need to value ourselves and each other and the kingdoms upon which our life totally depends. Without the plants, the insects, the animals, we have no existence. (It is rightly humbling to remember that our existence is dependent upon the garden worm who makes soil for the plants!) Without a new dream, we will exterminate ourselves and do great damage to other kingdoms. Waking up now is essential.

# THREE

# INTRODUCTION to the Medicine Wheel

In shamanism the word 'Medicine' means vital force – energy which is inherent in nature. A person's *medicine* is their power, their knowledge, their expression of their life energy. A Medicine Wheel is a circle of power, of knowledge, of understanding. The Medicine Wheel teaches us the balance and relationship of all things:

> *Our teachers tell us that all things within this*
> *Universe wheel know of their Harmony with*
> *every other being, and know how to giveaway*
> *one to another, except man. Of all the Universe's*
> *creatures, it is we alone who do not begin our*
> *lives with knowledge of this great Harmony.*
>
> HYEMEYOHSTS STORM, *SEVEN ARROWS*, BALLANTINE, 1972

Since antiquity Medicine Wheels have been used for teaching about the cosmos. The remnants of stone circles can be found all over the world. The ancients saw their world in terms of circles and cycles and time as circular rather than linear. Medicine Wheels teach of how the natural order works, of the human's place in that order and of the purpose of life. They show the powers that hold the universe in balance. The Medicine Wheel system is a living, vibrant, teaching pathway and as such it changes and adapts to the needs of the people in their present time circumstances.

When teaching at workshops I have been challenged by people saying that I am teaching another belief system. But 'believing' is not the idea at all! The idea is to stimulate your own thought, intuition, seeing and feeling processes, to inspire you to come closer to your own spirit, to catalyse your imaginative faculties. There is only one guideline – does it work for you, does it touch your heart, does it help and guide your life? The only way to find out is to try it out. That way you gain knowledge instead of wasting your time on belief. Harley Swiftdeer, a Metis Medicine man, has some lovely plays on words and one of them is this. A 'believer' is someone who *be* in the *lie* for *ever*. It may not be etymology but it is a truth! So don't believe, do your own inner work till you know!

Now a word about teachers. All the native teachers I have met have Heyeokah qualities. A 'Heyeokah' is the Native American term for a contrary, a clown, joker, trickster, a coyote. Westerners often tend to approach teachers, gurus and so-called enlightened masters from a place of naive trust. This can be a bad mistake, as numerous seekers have found out to their cost, in terms of money, self-development and power. They found they were empowering, developing and enriching the guru, not themselves. A good question is 'Does your teacher have a sense of humour? And does that sense of humour extend to him or herself?' Humourlessness is a sure sign that you should head for the door.

A student who gives total and naive trust gives away all power and self-responsibility. Such a student effectively goes to the guru and says 'Do it to me!' The guru's job is then just that. To take the disciple for a massive ride until he or she takes her power back. No real teacher wants a sycophant for a student. Monty Python's film *Life of Brian* has a hilarious scene where Brian, the accidental guru, cannot get away from a horde of horrendous followers who slurp on his every word. False teachers will happily take all you've got and laugh all the way to the ashram's bank. Real teachers will play tricks on you to get you to wake up and take your own power, claim the right to make your own choices and take responsibility for the outcomes. But they can be painful tricks – it is best not to give all your power away in the first place. Surrender does not mean submission.

A native, earth-connected person growing up in an old-style culture would be unlikely to have this problem in the same way as a Westerner. Not having been taught to believe parrot fashion in a separate god, not having learned a whole religion that depends on taking on without question a set of unprovable beliefs, not being disconnected from the earth, the native is more likely to approach the teacher as a guide who is further along the Great Journey, as a potential friend, as someone who is more deeply connected to the spirit world and the causal realm. Such a person is likely to have faith in the journey rather than naive belief in the teacher. Such a person is someone a teacher can begin the work with.

All the native teachers and elders I have had the good fortune to meet laugh a lot. All around them is humour, joking, clowning, bantering, teasing, deflating, a gentle knocking of any sense of preciousness. And educational practical jokes. That's what a Heyeokah does – trick you into your own growth! That's what life has done to you or you probably wouldn't be reading a book like this.

## POWERS OF THE NORTH

| | |
|---|---|
| Element | Air |
| World | Animal |
| Human Aspect | Mind |
| Human Shield | Everyday Adult |
| Time | Future |
| Enemy | Clarity (Bullshit) |
| Ally | Wisdom, Balance, Alignment, Knowledge, Harmony. |
| Colour | White |
| Manifestation | Philosophy, Religion, Science, Maths |
| Heavenly Body | Stars |
| Season | Winter |
| Totems | Buffalo / Wolf / Horse |

*The Knowing place*

## POWERS OF THE WEST

| | |
|---|---|
| Element | Earth |
| World | Mineral |
| Human Aspect | Physical Body |
| Human Shield | Adult Spirit Shield (Inner Priestess/Priest) |
| Time | Present |
| Enemy | Old Age & Death (Inertia) |
| Ally | Introspection, Intuition, Change, Death |
| Colour | Black |
| Manifestation | Magick, dance |
| Heavenly Body | Earth |
| Season | Autumn |
| Totems | Bear / Owl / Jaguar |

*The Looks-within place*

## POWERS OF THE EAST

| | |
|---|---|
| Element | Fire |
| World | Human |
| Human Aspect | Spirit |
| Human Shield | Free & Magical Child (Child Spirit Shield) |
| Time | Beyond Time |
| Enemy | (Misuse of) Power |
| Ally | Illumination, Enlightenment, Play, Medicine, Pleasure, Beauty |
| Colour | Yellow/ Gold |
| Manifestation | Art/ Writing, Media |
| Heavenly Body | Sun |
| Season | Spring |
| Totems | Eagle |

*The Sees far place*

## POWERS OF THE SOUTH

| | |
|---|---|
| Element | Water |
| World | Plant |
| Human Aspect | Emotions |
| Human Shield | Inner child |
| Time | Past |
| Enemy | Fear |
| Ally | Trust and Innocence |
| Colour | Red |
| Manifestation | Music |
| Heavenly Body | Moon |
| Season | Summer |
| Totems | Mouse / Coyote / Serpent |

*The Close-to place*

The Four Directions are the fundamental powers of the four cardinal points of the wheel. Grandfather Sun rises in the *east* and so is placed there along with the power of illumination, the fire of the imagination, the light, the Spirit – the non-manifest aspect of ourselves. As the great Fire which lights our lives, Grandfather Sun also brings us the element of fire, so that is also placed in the east, along with the colour yellow-gold and the kingdom of humans, we divine-mortals whose job is to determine and to caretake. The polarity here is masculine; the human shield is the free or magical child and the time is timelessness. The east is the *Far Sighted Place* and its totem is the eagle.

Mother Earth is placed across in the *west*. Mother Earth is dark and physical. From her all is born and through her all has life. Naturally, the element of earth is here and the kingdom of the minerals: the Stone People. The west is the place of the physical; for us it is the Body-Lodge which the Great Mother gives us to experience a three-dimensional life of choice. The time that the body understands is now. When we remember a joy or sadness, the body registers the remembered feelings as if they were in the present. The power we need to live on the earth is introspection, the ability to see deep within ourselves and also into the structure of life itself. The west is the *'Looks Within Place'* and its totem for most north Native Americans is the bear (hence teddy bears). The Inca totem is Jaguar who 'consumes our spirit at death' and returns it to the 'Great Round' unless we die awakened, in which case we can escape the mouth of the jaguar and walk the 'Rainbow Path Along His Back'. The enemy is death in that Mother Earth takes our 'Body-Lodge' back at the end of our time. The human shield of the west is the Adult Spirit Shield or inner priest or priestess, of opposite polarity to our everyday adult persona.

In the west our struggle is between on one side deep introspection, which brings us inner knowing and connection to the Primal Force which creates and is in All-Things; and on the other inertia, a feeling of being stuck, disconnection, living death. To dare to be truly alive and vibrant in every living moment is a daunting task. It means being true to oneself all the time – not avoiding things, not telling lies, not taking the easy way out of situations, not compromising one's truth. The colour of the west is black, and the polarity is feminine, receptive, creative. 'All Is Born Of Woman' is the first Great Sacred Law and it means many things. We go into our feminine place, our dark, solitary place to begin to create. Only when we have given birth to the new idea, the embryo, and then let it ferment into a concept, can we bring it out into the east, into the light of day. If an idea is brought out too soon before it is well composted in the darkness, it frequently dies. How many times have you talked and talked about something which you never got down to doing? It is probably better to keep quiet, get on with it and say nothing!

The Firstborn kingdom of Mother Earth and Father Sun is the plant kingdom. Plants thrive in summer heat and their existence is dependent on water so they are placed in the *south* (these teachings having originated in the northern hemisphere). The aspect of ourselves represented here is emotion – energy motion – and the shield is the Child Substance Shield, sometimes called the 'wounded child'. The time is the past because emotion relates to past events. The ally quality is *trust and innocence* and the enemy is *fear*: fear of being ourselves and acting our truth. There are two kinds of fear – Swiftdeer calls the first 'reality fear', the fear of a real threat, for example an earthquake. When we feel this fear we act without self-consciousness, self-doubt or any of those myriad human emotions that come out of past traumas and conditionings. Our being acts and that is it. We tend to feel that fear in the back of the neck. All other fear is by comparison 'unreal fear' which we feel in the solar plexus. That is the fear involved in showing ourselves, sharing ourselves, thinking we are being judged, doubting whether we are good enough and so on. This is the fear that our mask will drop and horror upon horrors, people will see us 'naked' for who we really are! All this fear is a by-product of our self-importance, and our efforts to develop a mask of social acceptability. I enjoy demonstrating this to groups or audiences by talking about the differences, meanwhile lowering my voice until everyone is listening intently and then suddenly producing a loud, horrible noise which brings about a moment of real fear!

To get beyond that and trust the universe, to have, in Biblical terms, 'faith in God', is the work of the *south*, the work of 'erasing personal history'. The south is called the '*Close-To Place*' and its totem is usually Mouse. It can also be Coyote the Trickster, who gets us into fine messes to help us wake up. For the Incas it is Serpent who sheds his skin and is thus a totem for the shedding of past conditioning.

In the *north* is placed the element of air, and the kingdom of the first air breathers, the animals, who developed the quality of mind. The mind thinks and plans for the future like the squirrel and her nuts, so future is the time of the north. The human shield is the Adult Substance Shield, meaning the everyday adult persona. The ally quality is wisdom, balance, harmony, alignment, knowledge – in other words, mind that is connected to the source. The inner or *nagual* enemy is mind that only thinks it is connected to the source, usually put as 'clarity'. This means know-all-ness. This state always makes me think of the old joke about heaven this way and philosophical lectures about heaven (and a long queue) the other way! We can differentiate the enemy and ally here: real inner wisdom is one way and lectures about wisdom – in other words bullshit – are the other way. I find when I use the native American word 'clarity' for this people get confused! But if I use the good, clear, simple word 'bullshit', everyone understands immediately. The colour associated with the north is white, the snow of the north, purity of wisdom and clear mindedness, the white hair of the elder. The north is the *'place of knowledge'* and its totem is Buffalo, or sometimes Wolf. For the Incas it is Horse, the keeper of the wisdom and philosophy of humans.

The *centre* of the wheel is the void, the non-manifest source from which all comes: the Egg, the Seed of Creation.

The Four Directions make a cross and it is this cross on which the 'Christ' is crucified. Each of us humans, as the potential Christ, the 'son/daughter' of God the Creator or Creatress, is 'crucified' on the cross of material existence. We are incarnated into the limitation and restriction of matter, in a body which requires a lot of looking after, which is frail and in its early years quite incredibly helpless. We are 'crucified' on the cross of earth, water, air and fire (body, emotions, mind, spirit) and we are 'victims' of our situation until in adulthood we 'turn our medicine wheel' by application of our will and focused intent. The cross without the circle is the cross of pain and suffering. The cross within the circle is the cross of the balance of joy and pain. The cross in a broken circle, the swastika, is the sign of the shaman who has 'turned the wheel' and become master of his or her own Circle Of Life. That is the ultimate purpose of these teachings and this path.

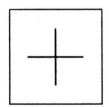 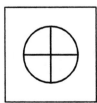 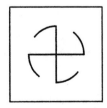

# *Our Journey*

Most of us begin our journey as an ordinary person under the thrall of everyday culture, governed by our needs for security, approval, recognition and acceptance – someone who relies on the outside world for a sense of identity and has given away an enormous amount of their personal power.

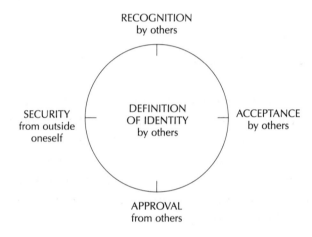

How sad it is that such a state of affairs should be considered 'normal'. When I am giving a talk I often ask the people how many of them have ever been in a trance or been hypnotized. Some hands go up. I then ask how many think they have never been in a trance, never been hypnotized. Usually quite a number of hands go up, some very firmly. I then ask 'But what about the trance you are in right now?' Often there is a laughter of recognition. I talk about the deepest trance state on planet earth – the one we know as normal waking consciousness! For some this is a contentious and challenging idea, but just how conditioned are you? Just how conditioned, hypnotized, entranced are others you know?

Ever since we plopped out of the womb, we have been subject to indoctrination. It is what we know as education, religion, upbringing, and it teaches us how to fit into the family and culture around us. Later in life we may travel to very different cultures and, if we stay long enough, get a sense of how they see the world. Then the chances are good that we will get a culture shock on our return home. This is a great opportunity to see just how 'normality' is a cultural phenomenon and not a given; to see just how odd and how selective is so much that our culture insists is normal, right and just.

As we grow up it is the family image-makers and archetypes who form our emotional understanding of the world. This is where our conditioning begins. Then in adolescence the peer group becomes all important and we are greatly influenced by the fashion industry and media at that time of our life. Most of us are desperate to belong, especially if our self-esteem is low, and so these types of influence can have enormous power in forming how we see and feel the world on the tricky transition from child to adult.

Our physical circumstances are governed by the economic image-makers, by those who control the wealth, and by the images put out of what it means to acquire wealth and the presumed freedom and happiness that we are led to believe results from that acquisition. The 'spiritual' aspect of life was controlled by the religious image-makers, the churches, who taught one what to believe. By giving over one's search and leaving it to them, believing what one was told, one could be 'saved' – from the difficult and rather nasty path of actually looking at oneself and having to take responsibility for one's own spiritual and psychological development! So self-discovery was, in a subtle way, taught as unnecessary.

WAY of

In the centre of this wheel are the political image-makers, those to whom we are taught to give away the most power. We can also place our sexuality here. You may think these make a strange combination! But our sexuality is the most creative part of ourselves. Through sex we create new life; only through sex is our race continued. Sexual power is located in our root wheel (or chakra) and the primal energy of sexuality is also our creative energy, our individuality. It is our sex that leads us on the merry dance of life, that pushes us out to meet and unite with others, that creates the mixing of peoples. Sex is the great stimulator and mover within each of us. Therefore it is the prime target of those who would seek to control us. There are two paths to world domination. One is with the 'sword' – the great empire-building, conquering armies – the other is with the suppression of sexuality, and that is called religion! An old joke says that what the Roman Empire failed to do in conquering Europe, the Roman Church completed. This is why all the major world religions have made control of sexuality a prime target. By creating sexual mores that set a person against their own nature and offering redemption only for those who comply, they can keep the people hooked in 'sin'. What a superb way to control the masses, so much cheaper than secret police, gulag camps and all that repressive government and police machinery. Just give them guilt and you can have them under your influence. It wasn't like that in the earth-based old world cultures where sex was celebrated as a great source of joy and creativity.

SOCIAL IMAGE MAKERS (PEER, BEER GROUP!)
MEDIA / 'MEANING OF LIFE'
Images of who you have to be in order to be 'in'
**MENTAL**

**PHYSICAL**
ECONOMIC IMAGE
MAKERS
AVAILABILITY OF
RESOURCES
Image of how
you need to be to
sell yourself
for a living

**RELATIONSHIP
& POLITICAL**
Images of how it is ok &
not ok to be sexual; & of
how you 'should' be to
have political voice

**SPIRITUAL**
RELIGIOUS /
CULTURAL IMAGE
MAKERS
ONE'S VISION
Image of what you
'should' worship to
be accepted in your
culture

**EMOTIONAL**
FAMILY IMAGE MAKERS & ARCHETYPES
Images of who you 'should' become
and how you should live your life

# *Basic Needs*

We all have basic needs and these are 'needs' not 'wants'. If we
don't have these, we don't survive. We need adequate food and
clean water, adequate shelter and clothing, adequate sleep and
dreaming. Experiments have been done in sleep deprivation which
have shown that without REM dreaming sleep, we lose our ability to
function. This dreaming sleep is our internal filing system that deals
with the day's experiences. We also need adequate 'knowledge' and
'medicine'. Without mind-food we become like zombies and lose
our 'Spirit' – our inspiration. We also need adequate free will and
orgasm. The wheel teaches that orgasm goes with free will, with our
ability to make our own decisions and determine our own life.

ADEQUATE SLEEP
& DREAMING

ADEQUATE
SHELTER &
CLOTHING

FREE WILL &
ORGASTICNESS

KNOWLEDGE,
HEALING &
MEDICINE

ADEQUATE
FOOD & WATER

# The Great Journey of Awakening

## South

Once we have understood all the concepts outlined above, we can step consciously onto the Great Journey. The first step is the South and is called with the humour of the *heyeokah* – 'Erasing Personal History'. Why humorously? Because it's impossible to erase personal history! Joan Halifax, author of *Shamanic Voices*, likes to call it 'embracing personal history', which makes a lot of sense and is less easily misunderstood. It is about erasing the negative controlling effects the past has on the present, and working through the old traumas, fears, addictions; the repressed anger, hate, resentment, grief; the sense of loss, the abandonments, betrayals, wounds. In today's parlance this means doing whatever psychotherapy is needed. Remember that psyche means soul and therapiea means doctoring, so we are talking about soul-doctoring, psycho-spiritual work, not just the limited field of what is often thought of as psychotherapy, psychoanalysis or psychiatry. To 'erase personal history' is to heal the emotional body so that one becomes an actor in the world, not a re-actor. With the great realization of the true nature of the emotional body, one gains mastery over the 'lower' self and is no longer run by the emotions, but is guided by feelings. Psychic abilities begin to open up as the confusing muddle of emotional needs, wants and addictions retreat to the sidelines as monsters that now become friends.

On the medicine wheel the South–North axis is the *Red Road*. This is the road of the heart, of the feelings, of the mind, of the soul. The West–East axis is the *Blue Road*, the road of body and spirit, of the depths and of the light. These make a wheel, a completeness. Unfortunately in the Western world they are only too often cate-gorized as separate – spiritual and psychotherapeutic work are considered as separate areas. From a shamanic point of view this makes no sense – psychotherapy (doctoring of the soul) is a spiritu-al undertaking, and spiritual work without healing the wounds of past trauma has no solid foundation. The shaman's journey is a holistic healing journey and involves all four directions, all four aspects of a person.

It is very important for Westerners to understand that emotional healing has two distinct stages:

## Get in touch with feelings

Open up to the buried pain and anguish locked away in one's past which, for so many, silently wreaks havoc with daily life and with health. This is painful, nitty-gritty work. The pain of the past will live on, hidden in the memory, in the musculature, until it is brought forth, re-framed, released and healed.

## Discipline the emotions

Only a child lives with uncontrolled emotions. It is now time to gain control of the emotional body, to feel your feelings but to have control of when and how you express them. I see a lot of problems from lack of understanding of these two distinct yet seemingly contradictory stages. At times it seems that Eastern spiritual paths teach only the second part and Western psychotherapy teaches only the first, so sometimes we get spiritual people with stiff upper lips and emotionally uncontrolled people in therapy!

## How others hold us in their image

Erasing personal history has another vital aspect and that is the image others have of us. Our family and friends will have a firm idea of who we are, of our abilities and our blindnesses, our talents and quirks. Once we start to grow and change, we will no longer play the same pain games with them and the chances are that at first they will get upset and try to put us back in the box in which they were accustomed to keeping us. These are battles that each one who steps onto the Great Journey must face. All spiritual paths have coded instructions which deal with the problem of losing friends and family and how this may be, to some extent at least, unavoidable. A person who has been a family scapegoat returns to the parental home after a time of growth and transition and all the old games are played out by the other family members, but the person no longer reacts powerlessly. The result is likely to be fear and anger on the part of the family. This person is not the son (daughter, grandchild, sister, brother, husband, wife and so on) that 'I' knew and what right have they to behave in this way? The warrior must stand firm no matter what. If the price is losing friends and family, then so be it, things can always heal with time. To give in is to lose a battle, and that battle will come up to be fought again and again. And each time it is likely to be more painful and difficult.

## The West

The second stage of the journey is the west and the name given to this stage is 'Meeting death as an advisor and ally'. This has many meanings starting with the basic one of remembering at a fundamental level that the body we inhabit is temporary and will one day be claimed by death. That does not mean that our consciousness ends, but that this incarnate journey ends. This opportunity for growth and development here in flesh on the Great Mother, living in the material world between the forces of light and dark, comes to an end. We go back to the Great Round, to the spirit world, to the world from which we came.

This also means facing the need for many pieces of ourselves, many of our current attitudes, ideas of self and so forth, to die. Death gives life. A person who gets stuck in life and resists change is holding on to redundant aspects of themselves. The only thing that is constant on this earth is change, and when we resist it we get stuck and go 'dead' – ultimately into depression. The quality of the west is deep introspection – the 'Looks Within Place'. In the west we move beyond the personal history of the south place and into our place of cultural healing. We are not islands, we are part of our family, village, tribe, city, country and ultimately all humanity and all of planet earth.

When we introspect deeply we touch into the archetypal world and we can begin to see what forces are playing themselves out through us. With a deep inner world connection our intuition grows. Intuition is connection with the spirit world or realm of cause. It is the realm where we can 'know' things and begin to dispense with having to believe what others would have us believe. Thus we move forward on our journey to self-determination and individuation.

## The North

The third point on the journey is the north, the realm of the mind, and here the movement is called 'Stopping the World' (or, in Zen, 'direct knowing' or 'unobstructed awareness'). This means stopping the everyday 'trance state' of normal waking consciousness which tells us that the world is 'out there' and is happening to us, and meeting the inner realm of cause, of mythology, of spirit, which shows us, sometimes quite frighteningly, that this is where it really happens and that, in fact, the world out there is but an echo.

## East

The fourth movement is the east of the wheel and is called 'Controlling the Dream'. This movement is also to 'seek new vision and purpose'. All that manifests in the third dimension of everyday reality happens first in the 'dream', which is the fifth dimension. It is time to quest for vision and seek direct connection with the dream world, the causal realm and its spirit teachers, to clarify intent for life so one can dream it awake. It is time to dare to awaken to knowledge of real reality – to the way things really are.

## Centre

The last movement is to the centre to assume full responsibility for one's existence and step into power. There is no longer anyone or anything to blame. It is time to take full responsibility for all your actions, but without guilt or shame. Life is a perfect balance of light and dark, an arena for learning and growing into illumination and enlightenment, guided by the spirit, living in trust and innocence; a child again but this time a magical child.

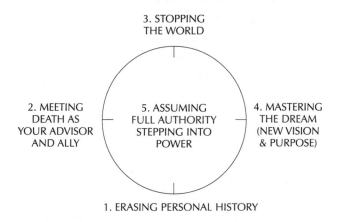

*The Great Journey*

# Tools to Help and Guide Us On The Journey

In the south we have mythology, teaching stories about the archetypal stages and battles of life. We have 'soul doctoring' which includes psychotherapy, hypnotherapy and all ways of healing the wounds of the emotional body.

In the west we have ceremony. Ceremony often makes little sense to the rationalist, stuck in his Newtonian description of the universe. However, ceremony is a powerful way of speaking to the Inner Being. Through enactment in the outer world, such as by setting up a Medicine Wheel with stones, marking the four directions, and then facing the directions to make prayers and to physically connect with water, earth, air and fire, we can convey information to our Inner Being. Just as our Inner Being (so wrongly called *sub*conscious or worse still *un*conscious – *mega*-conscious would be a more accurate name!) speaks to our Outer Being in the language of the dream world, so we need to use that same language to speak from the outer to the inner. Ceremony is the perfect vehicle for this. Our Inner Being receives the experience of a ceremony as both real and happening *now*. Thus it is such an effective way to change the 'dream'.

Affirmations have become quite popular in the last 20 years. The drawback for me is that they tend to use verbal language that the outer consciousness fully understands but which is not the natural language of the inner self. The joy with ceremony is that it uses dream enactment and thus can communicate more directly to the Inner Being. A good ceremonial leader uses lots of trappings and theatre to get the message past the everyday consciousness, to distract it while the real message goes in. In a sense it is three-dimensional hypno-drama-therapy!

Also in the west of the Medicine Wheel we have earth awareness and dance and movement. These are ways of getting to the earth of ourselves. If we consider a human as centred in the heart chakra, the lower world or earth world is all that is below – the solar plexus centre, the hara, and the root chakra. The upper world is all that is above – the throat, the third eye and the crown. The west relates to all that is below (and the east to all that is above), and so the tools are to help us heal the wounds to our earth connection.

The North is the realm of the mind and so we have Medicine Wheel teachings – ways to help us to 'see', understand and 'frame' our world – and we have council – the sacred circle in which we share our inner life with each other and get to hear how it is for others inside themselves. We can place shamanic journeys and soul retrieval here as part of the movement of 'stopping the world', or we could place them in the west with the body and deep introspection. Always remember a Wheel is a map, not the territory, and stay flexible.

The east is the place of the magical child and of rebirth so here we have play – 'purposeless' creative activity – and vision quest, the placing of oneself in the natural world to receive vision from spirit.

In the centre is the greatest of all teachers – the Great Mother, Mother Earth, Mother Nature.

COUNCIL
MEDICINE WHEEL
TEACHINGS
SHAMANIC JOURNEYS /
SOUL RETRIEVAL

CEREMONY
MEDITATION
DANCE &
MOVEMENT
EARTH
AWARENESS

MOTHER
NATURE

VISION
QUEST PLAY
(purposeless
creativity)

DOCTORING THE SOUL
(PSYCHOTHERAPY)
'INSIGHT STUDIES'
PERSONAL MYTHOLOGY

*The Tools*

Now with these tools and understandings we can begin the path to become a Warrior of the Spirit. We can begin to work towards freedom, individuality, autonomy and authenticity, towards free will to choose the path of our life in the great search for the Mystery Of Self and Life.

That is the briefest of introductions to this multi-layered, multi-faceted teaching. The foundation medicine wheels are the Twenty Count or Children's Count, and the Star Maiden's Circle. These and many other wonderful teachings will have to wait for another book!

# FOUR

# A PRACTICAL
# Set of Tools
# for Shamanic
# Living

# *The Circle*

The ancients met in circles and thought of their world in the form of circles, hence their teachings often take the form of wheels. A circle suggests equality. Each member views the circle from a different place. Everybody faces inward with the same ratio of those on the same side of the circle to those on the opposite side. In the western way we meet in the square or rectangle with the teacher, priest or director up front in the superior position, usually on some form of raised platform, while the rest sit in rows ready to listen to what they are told. These arrangements perfectly echo the cosmology of the respective societies. For the westerner the Creator is separate, aloof, in charge and brooks no argument. For the ancient the Creator is here and all around, in everything and within and without the circle. For the westerner, knowledge is something taught by those who know to those who don't, who take it in the form of beliefs and attitudes to be followed and obeyed. For the ancient, knowledge is to be exchanged and shared as an ongoing revelation, each member of the circle having their place of value and expertise to share.

It is really good for us westerners to experience meeting in the circle and getting together in a sacred way. By sacred I mean meeting in a way which honours the Creator, Creatress, Creation, where each individual is honoured and there is the minimum of hierarchy. (This is the antithesis of the typical meeting in the pub where competitive 'alcohol consciousness' usually holds sway: the quick put-down, the snide remark, the subtle game of one-upmanship, the whole 'tabloid consciousness'. All this keeps the sacred far away and reinforces feelings of 'normal' self-doubt, lack of self-esteem and lack of self-love, thus engendering the need to compete and prove oneself. In such a situation try telling your 'friends' that you really like, appreciate and love yourself, and wait for the hurling of embarrassed abuse that follows!)

# *Ceremony and Ritual –*
# *Sacred Space and Time*

Ceremony and ritual are ways of creating sacred space and time, when normal ways of relating are put aside in order to honour something special. Ceremonies are ways of enacting something in the outer world which will speak to the inner being and the inner world. Normality is suspended, through the agreement of all concerned, and together we go into sacred time and place. We suspend the dominance of the ego and put aside 'busy-ness'. Sacred time is a time with no 'getting', no 'doing', no achieving, no trying. We can listen, speak our truth, pray with an open heart to the Great Powers of the Universe, deeply hear others in the circle. We can enter the magical place of timelessness in which here and now is all that is important. When the Hopis plant corn they do so in sacred time and space. They turn an ordinary act into a sacred act through their intention and focus.

Ceremony is a way to give energy back to Mother Earth and to hear her voice and the voices of her great powers. The Bible talks of Jesus speaking to the waves and telling the sea to be still, talking to the earth and doing the sort of things shamans regularly do. And he says 'These things that I do you can do also and greater things in my name.' Here 'in my name' means 'in my nature' – the nature of an Enlightened One. For a much deeper look into the nature of ceremony and ritual, I recommend Malidoma Patrice Some's *Ritual – Power, Healing and Community*, Gateway Books, 1996.

# *Altar*

An altar is a place where we are reminded of our origins in spirit, a place where we lay out in the material world objects which signify experiences in the spiritual world. The most formidable altar I have seen is don Eduardo Calderon's mesa, which I saw when I went on my journey of initiation in Peru in 1986. He began constructing it by carefully laying out a dirty old piece of rag! I was told later this was a precious piece of ceremonial cloth that had been handed down for hundreds of years from shaman to shaman. The mesa took him about an hour to set up and contained a surprising number of objects. It had three fields – on the left the 'campo ganadero', the field of the dark, on the right the 'campo justiciero' or field of the light, and in the centre the 'campo medio', the field of balance. Don Eduardo said it is important not to look at light and dark as positive or negative; that it is what we humans do with these forces that makes them good or evil.

Along the front of his altar he placed 13 staffs including the sword of St Michael, used to cut through spiritual obstacles, the staff of the hound dog which helps to find lost people or objects, and the staff of the eagle, used for acquiring vision and diagnosing illness. In the centrepiece was the staff of the serpent which balances the fields of light and dark and represents the bringing together of earth and cosmic energies. On the campo ganadero was the staff of the maiden, symbolising medicinal flowers and herbs, and the owl which represents ancient burial places and the forces of the night. On the far left was the staff of Lucifer, representing all aspects of evil.

For one's own altar it is good to start really simply with objects that 're-mind' you of meaningful, power-filled times that have taken you beyond yourself, beyond who you thought you were up to that point. When you gaze at your altar it should help guide you into a higher state of consciousness, to a feeling of connection to the Source; your Source.

## Incense

Incense is used all over the world, by traditional cultures, by churches and religious groups everywhere, to purify a place, a person, an object. The incense and the ritual differ but the aim is the same – to prepare the people and the space for sacred ceremony. The North Americans traditionally use a mixture of sage and cedar to do what they call 'smudging' – to purify everybody and everything involved in the forthcoming ceremony by wafting sweet smelling smoke around them. The shamanic explanation goes like this: sage banishes negative energies, spirits, thought forms; cedar balances the energies; and sweetgrass or lavender or pinon pine, or whatever else may be included, blesses all present. The scientific explanation is that burning herbs in this way banishes positive ions (those are the negative ones produced by electric current around trains, polluting fumes and so on), and encourages negative ions which are the positive life-affirmative ones found, for example, around flowing water (the scientists must have had a field day naming them back to front!)

When beginning a workshop or sacred gathering I like to 'smudge' the space with incense and a feather wand before the people come in, and then pass the smudge and wand around the circle for everyone to be cleansed individually. To do this, put a small quantity of the herbs in an earthenware bowl or a shell (abalone shells are wonderful) or use a pre-made smudge stick. Make sure it is well-lit and waft it around with the feather, bathing the people in the smoke with the clear intent in your mind of clearing, cleansing and blessing. This also gives a message to each individual that they are honoured and valued without having to prove anything. I also like to chant and drum with the group before starting work because that helps put the people into a mild altered state of consciousness where they are more receptive to the subtle realms and can more easily leave behind the outside world they have just come from. Expressed in a native way, it helps to banish 'bad spirits' or negative thoughts. It also helps me to do the same within myself and puts me into a mild 'trance' state. I put it in quotes because *you cannot go into a trance without coming out of the one you are already in!*

Normal waking consciousness is a 'trance' state and is just one limited state of awareness. It is the one which is most governed by the culture you are brought up in and live in. It is about the way you were taught to describe 'reality' and the way you have become accustomed to describing it and sharing this consensus agreement with others. It is not the only reality!

## *Talking stick*

When meeting in a circle, the tradition of the talking stick or stone (or any suitable object) is a good way to assist sharing from the heart. By passing the talking stick around the circle each member can be heard in turn. This facilitates everybody hearing everybody else. When a person holds the talking stick they are – to put it in a western way – speaker of the meeting for that period. They hold sway until they pass the stick on. The stick goes to everybody so everybody gets their turn to be heard, to be received by the others, to be validated. This means the shy and quiet get equal opportunity. Perhaps one of the greatest challenges of the talking stick circle is to learn to stop rehearsing what you are going to say and trust yourself in the moment. Many times I have watched the energy of anxiety travel around a circle, usually preceding the talking stick by about four to five places! An alternative to passing the stick is for each person to place it in the centre after their turn. Then whoever is moved to do so can pick it up next. A central fire, altar, or tray of candles makes a point of focus and helps remind us that it is the centre we are seeking.

## Prayer and meditation

Prayer and meditation are two sides of one coin. Your prayer is a communication from your self in the manifest world to the spirit world. Similarly, meditation is a way to open the door to communication from the other direction. There are a multitude of ways to do either. Prayer and meditation can include singing, dancing, drumming, humming, eating, walking – anything done with respect, awareness and conscious intent. In one sense we are praying all the time and even when we get into negative states and blame and complain, we are still 'praying'. The problem is that unconscious prayers like that are also heard and also bring results! Frequent statements like 'Oh typical me, I always get the wrong end of it', or 'If anything can go wrong, you bet it will go wrong for me' are, however unintentionally, self-fulfilling prayers. Watch out because the universe hears them too!

## Drum and rattle

The drum is the most important tool in the shaman's armoury. The monotonous beat of the drum is used for journeying by so many tribes – in all the Americas; in Siberia and many places in the old world; in Africa, with all its amazing rhythms, tones and effects for dancing, moving and healing the psyche through movement; in the power drumming of Japan, revived by bands like the Kodo drummers. Many consider the drum the single most consciousness-moving, healing artefact in human life. While the drum takes care of the lower vibrations, the rattle and countless variations of shakers do the same for the higher vibrations. Our consciousness responds to rhythm and sound and is deeply affected by it. (*More on the drum in Chapters 5 and 6*).

## *Invocation*

To begin any ceremony or ritual, the first thing after smudging with incense is to invoke the archetypal powers of the four directions. This is not just a native American way, nor it is limited to any particular culture. In the world of the ancients, the concept of the four directions is universal. The powers may be in different directions in different cultures, but that doesn't matter because this is a map of relationships, not absolutes. We invoke the great powers of the universe that they might bear witness to our endeavours, and help us banish ego and cross over into the place of oneness of self and All-That-Is. Invocation is a way of tuning our consciousness to the greater impulses of existence, and focusing on an agreed intent for a sacred time together.

A simple way to invoke the powers of the directions is to start in the east and call to the spirit of the rising sun for new beginnings and possibilities, for expanded visions for the people. Then invoke the south, calling for the warmth of noontime to warm the hearts of all present and bring a feeling of trust and innocence. Then the west, calling for the power to look within and be with the truth that resides there; then the north, inviting the calm of night and the benefit of wisdom and knowledge. Then call All-That-Is-Above and All-That-Is-Below and lastly the Creator/Creation.

If one is about to do a ceremony such as a Vision Quest, which is about moving from everyday earth consciousness, the most dense, to air, the least dense, then it might be appropriate to start with the west and work around the wheel to water in the south (which is the next less dense), to fire in the east, and then to air in the north. This progression acknowledges a movement from the solidity of earth to the potential of flying on the wind.

Alternatively, starting in the south one might call the element of water, the oceans, rivers, clouds; the plant kingdom, the trees, grasses, flowers; the healing power of trust and innocence to heal the past and the wounds of the child within, and to help you walk through the barrier of fear.

Call the west: Mother Earth, the mineral kingdom, the quality of 'Looks Within', of introspection, to help you challenge inertia and deadness; call for physical healing if needed.

Call the north: the element of air, the four winds, the animal powers and especially your own power animal. *(See Chapter 5.)* Call the powers of wisdom and knowledge to help you sort truth from fantasy and keep your mind open and unprejudiced.

Call the east: the element of fire, the world of our brother and sister humans, the presence of the magical child and of the power of illumination. Call for inspiration.

After calling the four directions, call All-That-Is-Above, and All-That-Is-Below; and lastly All-That-Is, the Creator, Wakantanka, God – whatever name means most to you. At the completion of your ceremony always remember to thank the powers for being with you and make some form of give-away.

There are countless ways to call in powers and it is best to let yourself be moved by the moment once you have a clear idea of what you want to bring towards you. There is only one way of calling that for me doesn't work at all, and that is when someone repeats parrot fashion what they have learned from a book or a manual. Then the heart, the spontaneity, and everything of value goes out of it. A real call-in, stumbled through by a beginner with heart and humour, is infinitely more valuable than any 'perfect' call-in learned and remembered by a 'wannabee' trying to be an 'expert'. The same goes for anything spiritual, it must come from the heart or it is dead!

In the uncompromising words of the mystic Meister Eckhart: 'All deeds which do not flow from your Inner Self are dead before God.'

## Fasting and feasting

Fasting is one of the most basic and ancient ways of taking oneself into sacred space and time. To consciously make the choice not to feed the body, to shut down wants and desires, to close off to earthly needs, opens the door to communion with Spirit. Fasting is a part of the Vision Quest, the Sun Dance and countless rituals all over the world. By quieting the body, we get to reach Spirit. After the fast is over comes the feast and thanksgiving. All things must balance out for harmony and peace.

## Sacrifice – making sacred

When I was in Morocco learning from the Gnawas I attended their all-night ceremony, the Derdeba. The Gnawas are descended from the West Africans brought north two or more centuries ago as slaves. They blended their African ways with the Sufi way which had come from the Middle East, and the result is a wonderful shamanic-flavoured teaching and some amazing trance-inducing music. The Gnawas play a stringed bass instrument called a Gumbri and crude metal castanets on which they produce the most extraordinary mind-moving rhythms to underpin their glorious singing. The Derdeba is their principal ceremony and it starts with the sacrifice of a sheep and three chickens.

We in the west have a very odd attitude to sacrifice which probably comes from having meat ready killed, bloodlessly wrapped in plastic and laid out in the butcher's shop or supermarket. We are separated from the act of taking the animal's life, yet eat the result without thinking. Many meat eaters would be appalled at the idea of sacrificing an animal. Yet that has been done to every animal that ends up as meat! Unfortunately it has most likely been done in a slaughterhouse without honouring – sacrificing – making sacred – the animal. At the Derdeba I watched the slaughter of the sheep and then the chickens, which was performed with honour, with prayers for their spirits and thanks for their give-away. Indeed my stomach turned a bit at the deaths, but I happily ate the meat they had given, with thanks.

Sacrifice means 'making sacred'. Something is given so that something may be received. The animal's life is given so the people may be fed. To receive we must be willing to give. Vegetarians please note – if you do not kill animals you kill vegetables just the same. If you don't, you die. Everything dies so something else may live, and we will die too and give-away our bodies which may become food for worms and thence perhaps grass. Then, who knows, a cow eats the grass and what was once 'me' is now cow! The cow becomes beef and so the circle goes around. This is the law of Mother Earth. She does not give forever, she lends. Our bodies are made from the substance of the earth and at the end of our time will be given back. Nothing is lost, just transformed from one thing to another.

*65*

## Fire ceremony

This is a 'give-away' ceremony and it is about the transformative effect of fire. Look into yourself and see what you are ready to let go of, including those aspects of yourself that you feel hold you up on your evolutionary journey, any addictions you may have and so on. Also look at and list your talents, abilities, gifts. In the ceremony you can, if it feels right to you, offer them in service of Great Spirit. The mythology says that if you truly give away unconditionally all that hinders you, if you give away conditional love – love as normally experienced – and if you put your offerings into the fire with pure heart, then those gifts that the spirit wills for you will be returned to you tenfold. But you must be totally unconditional – no conditions, no expectations whatsoever – especially tenfold ones!

Then you need a fire! This can be as simple as a candle, although a real fire brings one into a greater feeling of contact with Mother Nature. First set your scene. Smudge yourself – or selves if you are with others. Then call in the powers, especially the fire spirits who you are asking to work for you in this case. Then perhaps sing a chant or two or drum and rattle for a bit, to bring a sense of harmony and enhance the feeling of entering sacred space and time. Next prepare the fire by making an offering of essential oil or tobacco or something that feels good to give. Chocolate also makes a good offering and is a Mexican tradition. Ask the fire to accept your give-aways and transform the energy that has become stuck, or negative. For the moment of give-away, place yourself to the west of the fire. The ceremony is a way of passing a message from the manifest realm of the west to the spirit realm of the east. You are making a very specific and clear statement of intent. Make your offering to the fire with your prayers and see it burn up completely. Then pass your hands through the fire and bring them to your third eye, repeat and bring your hands to your heart, repeat again and bring them to your belly – your second chakra or hara. This enacts bringing the divine flame to your spirit, your heart and your body/mind. At the completion be sure to give thanks to the spirit world.

On my journey in Peru with don Eduardo, he said this is a good ceremony to do every full moon and suggested to us we should be sure to do it for the next thirteen moons. I did – and have done a ceremony almost every full moon ever since. That's 10 years now. I guess that was the idea – typical shamanic trickery!

## Sweatlodge ceremony

The sweatlodge is probably the most ancient way of cleansing known by humans on the planet. Through the ceremony of the sweatlodge one is cleansed and purified physically, emotionally, mentally and spiritually. While the sauna is a derivative of the sweat-lodge of the ancient Scandinavian peoples, the most familiar sweatlodge is in the style of the plains Native American people, although it seems very likely that forms of sweatlodge were prac-tised in most, if not all, parts of the old world. The lodge is constructed out of saplings bent and tied together to form an upside-down saucer shape, half a sphere. This is then covered with old blankets, tarpaulins and whatever is available until it is dark inside and reasonably well-insulated. For the Native Americans, the residents of 'Turtle Island' – the old name of all the Americas – the lodge symbolized the turtle, with the lodge being the body and the altar outside the door being the head.

A fire is built in a special way outside the lodge, about 10 to 15 feet away, usually to the east. A base is laid of logs, preferably about 6 to 9 inches in diameter, and then kindling and small pieces of dry wood are laid on top to form a flat surface. The rocks, which need to be volcanic in origin to withstand the heat, are laid in a cone shape on top. A nice way to do this is for all who are to sweat to place the rocks ceremonially one by one with a prayer. Around this cone is placed more wood to cover the rocks and provide a draw to pull the fire up from the base. It takes between about an hour and a half to two hours for the rocks to heat, by which time the fire has burnt down from the cone shape and the rocks can be removed. A pit is dug in the centre of the lodge into which the hot stones will be placed. Outside the door to the east an altar is created out of the earth dug from this pit and a spirit trail is laid with corn pahoe (or ordinary flour will do), connecting the fire to the altar and then to the pit.

In some traditions the lodge chief enters the lodge to bless and awaken it with sage and cedar and sometimes with the sacred pipe, to pray and invoke the powers. In other traditions a woman has this task as the lodge is the womb of the Great Mother. The people prepare themselves and line up to be blessed with smudge prior to entering the lodge. The door is always made low so one crawls in on all fours and it is traditional to make a prayer on entering saying 'For all my relations', or in native language, 'Omitakuaye Oyasin'. This is to emphasize that I sweat not just for myself but for all to whom I am related – all of creation. By purifying myself I affect all things for the better. The sweatlodge is seen as the womb of Mother Earth and the ceremony as one of entering the darkness, purifying – dying a little – and then coming out at the end cleansed of the past and reborn.

The people sit around the central pit, close together in this small dark space. The rocks are brought in and blessed with sage, firstly seven rocks symbolizing the Four Directions of the manifest world, the Above and the Below, and finally the Creator, WakanTanka, All-That-Is. The door is closed when there are enough stones to give the right temperature, everyone is ready. The lodge chief calls in the powers, making an offering of water to the rocks at the end of each prayer. There are many traditional ways of praying in a sweatlodge. The one I am most familiar with starts with a first round of prayers for oneself. It is considered vital to start with oneself as until one is healed and in balance, anything one attempts to do for others will be tainted with one's own needs and imbalances. The people pray one by one in turn in a sunwise circle. The chief puts an offering of water on the rocks at the end of each prayer so that it is carried in the steam to the Spirit World. At the end of the prayers, often a chant or two will be sung, and then the round ends, the door is opened and drinking water is passed around. More red hot glowing rocks will be brought in and then the second round begins. This follows the same ritual, except this time the prayer is for others, for anything and anybody except oneself.

The third round is prayers of the give-away, an opportunity to pray to let go of aspects of oneself that are troubling, that one feels ready to change, addictions one wishes to break free from, and perhaps also to offer one's gifts and talents in service of Spirit. The fourth round has no set form and is a time to listen. Hence it might be a silent meditation, a journey to the land of the power animals, or a time of chanting or toning together. At the end the chief gives thanks to the powers, often pours rather a lot of water on the rocks until the lodge is decidedly hot, until finally the door is opened and we come out looking somewhat pink and childlike and dive into the water if there is a nearby stream, or just lie on the ground.

Ed McGaa Eagleman described it thus:

*While the sweatlodge itself is simple to describe,*
*it is beyond any mortal writer's ability to*
*adequately convey the ultimate culmination of*
*spiritual, mystical and psychic expression of the*
*sweatlodge ceremony. You have to experience*
*it to truly realise its fullness and depth.*

I have been asked numerous times by people who have never entered a sweatlodge, 'What is the difference between a Sauna or Turkish Bath and a sweatlodge ceremony?' My answer is that there is almost nothing similar except for heat and sweat! I have had this view confirmed by many newcomers at the end of their first sweatlodge experience.

I had an unusual experience back in 1987 at a sweatlodge at Grimstone Manor Centre in Devon. It was at a workshop by Harley Swiftdeer, though he wasn't chief of this particular lodge, and being a particular healing sweat rather than the community sweat I have described, it consisted of seven rounds instead of the more usual four, with the door being opened once only. I was supposedly one of the more experienced people and so was asked to go next to the fire pit which for this lodge was placed in the north east corner. Bill, another experienced person, was sitting behind me. About two thirds of the way through this very hot lodge, I was kicked suddenly from behind and he shot past me towards the door. He had momentarily fainted and fallen onto the hot rocks and burnt his leg. He was helped outside but, stalwart that he is, he came back in a little later, heavily bandaged, to complete the ceremony. Then, as we were nearing the end I experienced a moment when I could stand it no longer; suddenly, uncontrollably, I completely lost my centre in fear of death and burst forward right across the lodge chief and the water bucket, somehow pushing my way out through the door to lay down thankfully outside to recover. After a bit I began to wonder how I had got out so quickly – had I upset the water, had I damaged the side of the structure in my panic, had I wrecked the sweat for the others and how much humble pie would I have to eat for making a total fool of myself? Marius, who was one of the fire keepers, looked after me as I lay on the ground and I remember watching people coming out of the lodge. I started asking people what had happened and no one would tell me – it felt very strange. Surely everyone must have seen me burst out like that or at least been disturbed by my precipitate action. No one seemed to know anything! Was there a conspiracy of silence? Had I done something so bad no one would speak to me? Finally I got some sense out of Liz, another of the participants. She told me I was one of the last in the lodge, I seemed to have gone to sleep and had to be nudged to come out at all!

I remember it took me quite a long time to get my body heat back after that. It was September and quite warm but I huddled in blankets shaking involuntarily over the Aga in Grimstone's kitchen for over an hour while being given hot drinks by kind people. Then I sat in the Jacuzzi until about two in the morning before I felt whole again.

In the words of Stalking Wolf, the Apache Grandfather who taught Tom Brown and is immortalised in Tom's books *The Vision*, *The Quest* and *The Journey*:

> *You have felt the presence of the ancients, the*
> *expansion of self, and the peace. You know now*
> *what a true ceremony should be, for as you felt*
> *the power of the lodge, so too will others,*
> *regardless of belief. The sweatlodge speaks to all*

*peoples in the language of their own beliefs and
thus it becomes a universal truth. So, then, use
the lodge as a tool, a doorway for physical and
spiritual renewal and cleansing, a pathway to
expansion and a vehicle to the worlds of the
unseen and eternal.*

## Psychic abilities

Some shamans say that we have twelve senses, not just five. Every
one of us is psychic or we could not function in the world. Everyone
has hunches, feelings, vibes, intuitions, knowings, a 'sixth sense'. If
we didn't, we would fall over things, have accidents, be out of tune
with others, be a danger to ourselves. There is no such thing as
'extra sensory perception', it is natural extended or developed sensory perception which comes to all who take the trouble to work on
developing themselves. Everyone has the potential to drive a car but
training is needed to develop the skills. Some will become very
expert, some will be clumsy, and the majority will drive in an average way – so it is with psychic abilities. In the shaman's world there
is no such thing as the 'supernatural'. What scientists call supernatural is all that does not fit into their paradigm of reality because
they haven't yet figured out how it works! Developing these powers
is a natural part of the shaman's path.

## Bone game

The Native American Bone Game or Hand Game is a good example
of a children's game which is actually a psychic development training exercise! Here is a simple version of it which can be played by
two teams or by just two people.

You require two small bones or sticks, one of which is marked. You also need a number of counters, say three for each team. For a team game it is a good idea to have a master of ceremonies to oversee and control the proceedings.

The two teams then make wagers which need not be the same but need to be agreed by all players. This can be an enjoyable challenge in itself. Then it is decided which team is to hide first and which to 'see'. One team appoints a 'hider' to secretively place one bone in each closed hand while the other team chooses a 'seer' whose job is to guess and correctly identify the hand with the marked bone. The rest of the team members assist, in the one case to focus the energy to help the seer and in the other to be as disruptive as possible.

The teams meet either side of a line which no one must cross. They each place their counters on the ground. Once the game begins, no words must be spoken, though any amount of noise can be made. The one hiding the bone presents two closed fists to the opponents, one containing each bone, while team-mates do all sorts of disruptive nonsense on their side of the line. The seer on the opposing team attempts to divine which hand holds the marked bone, assisted by team-mates in any way. Once the seer makes a guess by pointing, the hider shows the bones. A win means the gaining of a counter and another opportunity to be the guessers. A lose means the opposing team get the next opportunity to guess. (For a more detailed description see *The Way of the Shaman*, Michael Harner, Bantam, 1982).

## Psychic protection exercises

I have found that many people who suffer in all sorts of seemingly emotional ways are partly suffering because psychically they are very open without realising it, and are unable to shut off from the influence of other people's emotional vibrations. They pick up psychic 'emotional garbage' and think it's their own problem. The ability to be able to close down is equally as important as being able to be open, especially now that many more people are starting to open up.

About ten years ago I was running a residential workshop and everything became quite high and surreal. This was great for what we were doing as we felt very connected to other worlds. However I clearly did not do enough at the end to bring us all back to every-day consciousness. One car carrying people back burst two tyres on the motorway. No one was hurt but the car hit the central reservation and got somewhat bent. Another participant put clothes in her dryer and it promptly caught fire, and several people had other odd experiences. It was a big lesson. The further out we go, the greater the need to come safely back. Everyday consciousness is the state we need to be back in before going home! One practice I have taken on from some Tibetan teachers is the ceremony of Holy Spirit Water! At the end of a workshop that has reached heights, a great way to bring everybody down to earth is with a glass of wine or a beer. A nice way is to take everyone on a closed eye meditation to the source of holy water – with a touch of Coyote humour here and there – and to secrete the wine and glasses into the centre of the cir-cle while they have their eyes shut and are thinking cosmic thoughts. Then at the appropriate moment – manifest before their very eyes the holy water!

The main way of staying protected from unwanted psychic influ-ences is to be well and truly grounded in your body, here and now. For some that is more difficult than others, so here are some ways which can help.

# Protection Meditations

## The Psychic Cross

Imagine there is a cross running through your body. Your spine is the vertical component, your outstretched arms are the first horizontal beam, and the third direction is front to back right through your heart centre. You are the centre of a three-dimensional cross. Now draw energy up your back and down your front in a circular motion, visualize strong energy pulsating around you. Next spin energy from your left hand, up over your head and down to your right hand, under your feet and around and so on. Feel both these pathways of energy moving powerfully around you. Then add the horizontal by passing energy from your left hand around your front, still at arms length, and on to your right hand and around your back. (It doesn't matter which way any of these energies go.) Now you have three circles of energy pulsing around you. Then let these three energies merge into an egg of energy around you and feel it getting stronger and stronger. Really feel it as a powerful shield, moving and pulsating all around you. Then suppose you are going out somewhere where you may become psychically or emotionally challenged and possibly drained, you turn the outside of your energy egg to mirror, so any unwanted energies, barbs, negative thoughts or suchlike will be returned to their source. You can still let in love and care, but you are protected against dark energies. Practise this to build up the thought form until it is strong enough to really protect you.

## Pyramid of white light

From a point about a foot above your head draw down to the ground one by one four corners to make a pyramid. It is a good practice to do the actions physically at first. Then fill the pyramid with white light. Feel yourself surrounded by the white light and protected by it.

## *Spiral*

My friend, teacher and facilitator Fiona Fredenburgh teaches this one and it is a very useful quickie. From a point beneath the feet bring energy up through the chakras to a place above the head. Then spiral it around you and down back to where you started. You can fill the spiral with light or colour, whatever feels best for you. If you run into someone around whom you tend to become drained, run the energy quickly down and up. Another friend, Trisha Wood, has a splendidly rude way of classifying people into two basic types. She calls the lively ones around whom you tend to feel good and uplifted *Pinkies,* and the ones around whom you tend to feel drained and energy-sucked *Hoovers*! All these exercises are great *Hoover* protection!

I had an experience some years ago which convinced me of the need to take care of myself in this way. I went to speak at a forum of what turned out to be competitive and jealous mystics! I went in a state of openness and naiveté expecting a typical New Age gathering – which would have been fine – but that was not what it was. As soon as I started my talk I was interrupted and I could see that a segment of the audience simply wanted to be combative. I speeded up my delivery, raised the level of voice and aimed at those people who actually wanted to hear me, which was in fact a majority of the 80 or so present. I went home afterwards thinking no more about it but to my surprise suffered from a strange sort of bad stomach for the next three days. I have been on stage often enough to recognize the effects of stage fear on my body and I knew it wasn't that.

Someone with knowledge had aimed darts at me and I had been foolish enough to go without protecting myself. Never again!

Later, talking with a friend who knew about this particular scene, I was told that there were a number of people present with quite a bit of knowledge but who were very wounded, angry and jealous. Also it seemed I had committed a major sin. In answer to a question I had replied 'I don't know'. Apparently their usual speakers never do that, they bluff their way through whether they know the answer or not!

# Fibres

This brings us right onto the subject of luminous fibres and the creative use of them. I have learned many things in my life by default, (which is a euphemism for my own stupidity!) such as the incident just related. Here is another such story. I was living in San Francisco, attending Antioch University. It was about a mile walk from my home, a wonderful community of nine fellow students on the corner of Pine and Laguna Streets, to the University, which was also on Pine Street but in the middle of the city. There were two hills along the way and walking to and fro I was encouraged by my friends to put out my fibres from my solar plexus/belly area to the top of the next hill and imagine a winch there which would draw me effortlessly up. Well, I didn't want to say anything – after all this was California – but the cynic in me was on top form. 'What a load of old...!' But I did it anyway and just kept playing with the idea. Some months later I was walking with a girlfriend who was about 15 years younger than me, up one of those steep hills you see on San Francisco posters, from Union Square to Pine Street at the top of the hill. Suddenly I realized she was no longer with me. I turned round

WAY of

to look for her and saw her about ten yards down the hill, puffing away exhausted. 'Hey, Leo, what are you trying to do to me?' she said mournfully when I got back to her. My fibres had been drawing me up the hill effortlessly but she was exhausted! That's how I first learned to respect the power of intent and subtle energies.

# Exercises on the Human Aura

There are many useful exercises to help validate subtle energy fields and here are a few to try. For the first one rub your hands together and then put your palms about ten inches apart and move them in and out until you feel the energy between them. Then try this with a friend. Then move your hands all around your friend's body at about three to ten inches distance and see what you can feel of their energy field.

## Exercise in pairs – the unbendable arm

Put your hand on your partner's shoulder, clench your fist, hold your arm straight and ask your partner to put both hands over your elbow and pull down while you resist. The pull needs to be gradual until you both get a sense of how much force is needed to bend your arm. Then imagine you are a fire engine or pump. You are rooted to the earth and are drawing water up and it is pushing through your arm and out of your fingers at high speed with tremendous force. Such force that nothing can bend your arm. Then place your arm again on your partner's shoulder, this time with the fingers outstretched, hold onto the feeling and the image of the pump strongly, and ask your partner once more to apply gradual force to bend your arm. You will need to apply a little muscle power, but will find you can relax and hold steady with much less effort than before.

## Changing weight and defying gravity

This is quite well known so you may well have seen it or tried it before. You need five people for this. One sits on a stool, the other four are there to lift that person. Two stand at the back and place one of their hands only under a shoulder and the other two stand at the side and place one hand under the nearest knee. They then attempt to lift the sitter off the stool, noting how much strength it takes, or indeed if it is possible at all. Then they place one hand after another in rotation flat on the top of the sitter's head, perhaps all left hands first followed by all right hands. The palms, which are an energy centre, should be on top on each other. Then everyone pushes down a little and visualizes drawing off the gravity so the person will become lighter. After holding like this for a minute or so together they all quickly try the lift again. The sitter should positively bounce up off the stool! This also works when the hands are spaced above the head like an electrical condenser, not quite touching. I remember meeting someone from a small fringe theatre company who used this method to lighten heavy props. They would put their hands together over a table, just for a moment, and intend the table to be lighter, then lift it up and it was!

## Exercise in pairs – dead weight

Stand with a partner of about the same weight as yourself. One grasps the other around the waist from the back and lifts to test their weight. The person being lifted then roots themselves into the ground by imagining hooks from their feet into the earth, or roots like a tree going deep down. Then the partner lifts again – if he can! There are many stories of oriental martial arts masters being amazingly adept at this.

## *Weakening and strengthening a partner's fibres*

I was shown this exercise by Alberto Villoldo on my first journey to
Peru in 1986. First test your partner's muscles by asking them to
hold out both arms horizontally, straight in front with the hands
together. Ask them to resist while you push down on their hands to
test their muscle strength. Then invite them to relax while you set
out to cut the vertical fibres around their stomach area. Intend that
your energy goes out from your extended fingers as you move your
hand side to side a few times across their stomach in the solar
plexus area. Then test their muscles exactly as before. If this exercise has worked, their strength will be noticeably less, both to them
as well as you. Then be sure to put them back together again. Ask
them to relax and this time move your hands vertically up and down
intending to rejoin the fibres that you cut. Test the muscles again
and they should be strong. Once you feel confident that this really
works, the partner being tested can use a protection exercise, and
you can use this method to test its effectiveness.

You can increase the effectiveness of the 'cutting' by adding sharp
sounds. Kung-fu and karate fighters use these kind of methods to
weaken their opponents in the moments before engaging in physical combat. I learned a lot from this about how easy it is to get
weakened by some contacts and how helpful it is to use protection
exercises before entering potentially difficult arenas. And of course
I forgot all about it when it came to the experience of the talk
mentioned a few paragraphs ago!

## *Exercise – winched up the hill*

This follows from my story of using the fibres in San Francisco. Next
time you are faced with a hill to walk up, imagine a winch at the top

and a chord from it to your solar plexus/hara area. Invite the winch to draw you upwards easily and effortlessly. At first it may make little difference, but persevere with the visualization at every opportunity until you train yourself to tune into this extra source of energy.

### Exercise – walk talk, walk small – walk tall

This is a good exercise alone or with a group. Walk around consciously feeling your walk and your connection to the earth. Imagine you are connected from the base of your spine to the centre of the earth, and from the fontenelle on the top of your head by a silver chord to the centre of the galaxy. Feel your oneness with all things and your rightness in being in existence as a loved and valued part of All-That-Is. Then drop all that and let yourself feel at your worst: separate, disconnected, uncared-for, neurotic, self-pitying and so on. Get a sense of how that feels, play with it and let it guide you about yourself. Then shake it off and return to walking tall and this time play with it and really call the best into and out of yourself. Spend enough time to really get a 'felt' sense of you as the best of you. Then remind yourself that you have a moment by moment choice as to how to be in the world. You are the dreamer of your own experience of reality.

# Crafts

A great way to externalize what is going on inside oneself is to make a shield or an object of some kind. Medicine shields are a tradition of the North American people and they are not about protection, rather a shield is a display of one's inner process. Pictures of Native American encampments often show a shield placed outside the tipi which depicts the spiritual inner life of its maker.

To make a Medicine Shield using the teachings of the Medicine Wheel, look at the powers of the Four Directions, and meditate on what each direction means to you. Another way is to journey (*see Chapter 5*) to each direction and see what images come to you. Then paint or draw the images on the shield. The shield itself can be as simple as a piece of paper. Or you could take a sapling of willow, ash or hazel (or any bendy wood available), make it into a circle and bind the ends together firmly. Cut a circular piece of leather or woven material to fit, make holes around its edge and stretch it across the circle of wood. Then wind a piece of string or strip of leather around it, binding the leather to the willow.

# *Vision Quest*

The Vision Quest is a part of Native American and other old world cultures. One fasts and prays in a sacred place on the mountain for up to four days and nights, praying for a vision, for an opening to the spirit world, for reconnection with the Creator and Creation; to truly cry out to Creation, to lay oneself fully on the line, to release all that is held inside, to bare one's truth to the universe... I recount a little of my first such experience in Chapter 7. The most famous Vision Quest is probably that undertaken by the great Shaman of Nazareth, where he had to struggle for 'forty days and nights' with great archetypal forces of power.

Stephen Foster and Meredith Little pioneered the Vision Quest for people of all races and all lifestyles. In their *Book of the Vision Quest,* (Bear Tribe publications) they write:

> *This is about the re-creation in modern times of*
> *an ancient rite of dying, passing through, and*

*being reborn. It is also the story of the efforts*
*of a small (number of dedicated people) to assist*
*urban and suburban people to go into the*
*wilderness to enact this ancient rite of passage.*

And from Heyemeyohsts Storm in *Seven Arrows*:

*The Vision Quest or perceiving quest is the way*
*we must begin this search. We must all follow our*
*Vision Quest to discover ourselves, to learn*
*how we perceive of ourselves, and to find our*
*relationship with the world around us.*

The traditional Vision Quest has three distinct movements. The first is *severance*, in which you prepare and open up to the 'inner stuff' of yourself, look at your life and your joys and sorrows, talents and addictions, and take yourself more and more inside.

The next stage is *threshold* when you leave the everyday world behind and you enter Sacred Time and Place. Again, from the *Book of the Vision Quest*:

*Now you stand alone in the Sacred Time and all*
*around you are the features of eternity. The*
*mountains mock your flesh and blood. They have*
*been here for a hundred million years. Their*
*incomprehensible age thunders down a symphony*
*of eternity for your ears, a symphony of stillness.*
*For an endless three (or four) days and nights you*
*will be unable to escape the silence.*

Finally there is *reincorporation*, the return. I have run short Vision Quests, just one day and night, since 1987, as part of the *Elements of Shamanism* course. I always remember one participant coming back in quite a temper saying 'That was 23 hours and fifty nine minutes of utter boredom and futility.' (It might have been ruder than that!) By the end of *reincorporation*, he had utterly changed his view and seen some things about himself and his life patterns only too clearly.

I told this story this year at the beginning of the follow-on vision quest week for *Elements* participants who wanted to do a two or three day quest. 'That was me,' said a voice. I had completely forgotten who had said it – but he was back for more, which speaks volumes for the transformative power of this work.

*Reincorporation* is a vital part of the quest. I find that it is in the hearing of other people's stories that one's own comes into focus. And it is in the telling of one's own story that all sorts of aspects become clearer and learning takes place, fruitfully, although not always comfortably.

One's own life, friends and culture can look different after a quest. One can be moved to make changes that one never thought of before. A sort of depression can come after you and try to hook you into a feeling of impossibility, a sapping of will. This is the time to stay strong. You had your time of vision, of seeing, now is the time for action and manifesting the changes in your life that are called for. This too is an important time, as old demons never lay down right away. Whenever we make a creative change or gain greater insight into our make up and into the Universe, all the old patterns will come haunting us like dragons in the night, seeking to re-establish themselves in their old home – you! Hold strong and determined and once they are convinced you really mean it, they will lay down and become your friends and allies. A pattern defeated, an addiction vanquished, is a friend for life, an inner strength.

# FIVE

# THE SHAMANIC
# Journey and
# Soul Retrieval

The shaman is often described as someone who walks with one foot in the everyday world and one foot in the spirit world. One way of moving from the everyday to the spirit world is by the classic shamanic journey or soul flight which lies at the heart of the way of the shaman. This journey is a way of finding answers to problems, information to help and guide one's tribe or group, or help with one's own life. The shaman journeys to meet with spirits who may be regarded as ancestors, gods, goddesses, elders, deceased shamans, angels, power animals or spirit guides, and who are seen as beings with great wisdom and power who are willing to help and guide the living.

The shaman is a cosmic traveller. In the words of Mercia Eliade from *The Archaia Techniques of Ecstasy*:

> *He commands the techniques of ecstasy – that is,*
> *because his soul can safely abandon his body and*
> *roam at vast distances, can penetrate the under-*
> *world and rise to the sky. Through his own*
> *ecstatic experience he knows the roads of the*
> *extraterrestrial regions.*

## Other Realities

Shamans divide non-ordinary reality into three other worlds, the upper, lower (or under) and the middle worlds. Each has its own characteristics and whilst each individual traveller initially experiences their own version, once one becomes a proficient journeyer it is amazing just how connected we all are at these levels. Shamanic journeying really blows the myth of human separation and shows just how much we really are all part of one. In workshops I find that participants learn remarkably easily how to enter another's lower or upper world and gain helpful information. My friend and colleague Howard Charing says 'When I journey on behalf of someone else, I journey to their personal map, their unique place in these other worlds, and when I do this every aspect of the journey is significant.'

The *lowerworld* is the place of instinctual knowing where our animal-like powers reside and where we can find practical, earthy help and guidance. The lowerworld is the land in which fairy stories are set. Seemingly violent, terrible things can happen yet no one is hurt and the 'dead' just rise again when they feel like it. Alice's Wonderland is here and many cartoons are based on this world – and we know how kids love 'violent' cartoons! Most helping spirits of the lowerworld take the form of animals, some take the form of humans, and some mythical beings. Generally speaking, the lowerworld appears just like a natural landscape does in this world. When journeying, everything one experiences is of relevance and has a symbolic or even a literal meaning.

The *upperworld* is the world of spirit guides, cosmic beings, great wise elders who usually appear in human form. Their help and guidance tends to be more general and philosophical and not as earthy or practical as that of the lower world. The light tends to be translucent and pastel coloured and there is often an ethereal feel. In travelling upwards, in order to get there one goes through a membrane which may appear like a cotton wool cloud.

One very important point. The upperworld is not in any way superior to the lowerworld, just as on the medicine wheel the east is not superior to the west. They are complementary and equal and one would not exist without the other.

The *middleworld* is both the everyday physical world that we live in, the world of ordinary reality, or in Mexican terminology, the tonal. It is also a parallel non-ordinary version of our world. It is where psychic phenomena, vibes, hunches, telepathy, extra sensory perception, thought forms, 'weird' happenings and so on, occur. This is the world where disease and sickness manifest themselves before moving into the physical body, the world where psychic healers work, and where psychic darts are thrown. To the shaman, it is preferable to seek a cure before getting sick! When one feels unwell or dis-spirited, it is good to go to the shaman and for him (or her) to take a look into your energy field, to see if any intrusions may be in there and then remove them. Oriental medicine rests on this same premise. The shamanic cultures see disease as a result of dis-ease caused by an invasive force acting against health. The Western idea of waiting until the physical body is sick before seeking help is, from a shamanic point of view, totally archaic!

The middleworld is a difficult place to navigate and one needs to be well experienced before attempting it. We pick up things anyway if we are not careful. (*See the Psychic Protection exercises in Chapter 4.*) Much the best place to start journeying is the lowerworld.

## The Drum – the 'Shaman's Horse'

To journey you need to enter an altered state of consciousness often called the 'shamanic state of consciousness', or SSC for short. The greatest way to facilitate this is with the 'shaman's horse' – the drum! A drum beat at a steady 200 – 280 beats a minute, approximately equivalent to theta brainwaves, helps to still mind-chatter and 'hold' you while you journey. I have seen many people in workshops who have previously been accustomed to guided visualization experience a great revelation the first time they journey with the drum. It feels so much more real. Of course, to a shaman, alternative realities are just as real as the everyday. When we journey we go to a real place and meet real power animals and spirit guides. For a Westerner to argue with an indigenous shaman about just what is really real is pointless! To understand a shamanic way of seeing, you have to enter the shamanic cultural understanding and way of framing the Cosmos. For a westerner to do that he has to change his cultural hypnosis completely, otherwise he is like someone discussing a Boeing and insisting it doesn't drive properly on a motorway, not realizing it is supposed to fly!

# Introductory Exercise to Journey to the Lowerworld

You will need a quiet place and either a friend with a drum or a shamanic drumming tape and personal stereo with earphones.

> *Smudge yourself or light an incense stick to help get yourself into 'sacred space' and lay down comfortably. Either cover your eyes or darken the room.*

> *For the first journey it is good just to visit and observe, so speak your objective out loud. 'I am journeying to the lowerworld to visit and observe.'*

> *Let your breathing slow down as you consciously relax your muscles and feel the gravity of Mother*

*Earth holding you. Then visualize a place you
know from which you can easily imagine
travelling down into the earth. It might be a
hollow tree, a disused mine shaft or well, the
bottom of a lake or ocean, even an underground
railway tunnel! Let yourself 'be there' and as the
drumming starts, enter the tunnel which will take
you into the earth. Firstly you will meet the
'guardian of the lowerworld' and if it is a good
day to travel, the guardian will let you through.
(If not, return and try another day.) The tunnel
will slope down and will probably become steeper
as you go. Let it carry you down, down, down;
deeper and deeper into the earth. If you come
across an obstruction, just go round it or find
a gap through. Continue down until you find
yourself outside in a natural landscape. You may
come to a cave and if so, follow the path out into
the landscape. Look around you and examine
what is there. Nearby is your own personal power
place. Go there and look around. Be aware if it is
day or night-time, sunny or raining, still or
windy; if you are in forest, open meadow, barren
wasteland, gentle woodland. Are you near
running water, is the land fertile or desert, can
you hear birdsong and are there animals around?
While exploring the landscape, keep track of
where you are, and when the call-back comes,
return to the cave or entrance to the tunnel and
return. Make a note of your experience.*

# Power Animal Retrieval Journey

*Take the same journey described above but this
time state your intention clearly to meet and
retrieve your power animal(s). When you get to
your personal power place, call your animal(s) to
come to you and wait and see what happens.
When an animal comes, to be sure it is your
animal look in the four directions. If the animal
shows up all four times, you can be pretty sure it
is for you. If you are uncertain, ask the animal
straight. It will give you a truthful answer or
indicate by body language. (Remember that in
the dreamworld we communicate with dream
language, not linear words which are an
invention of the third dimension.)*

*When you have made contact with your animal –
and it may be a bird, a mythological animal, or
it might appear in human form, but it is not
considered good for it to be an insect, call the
animal to you and when the drum sounds the
return, bring it back with you in your arms to
this world.*

A friend had a journey where a Landrover appeared! He looked at it
afterwards in the same way one would look at any image. What did
it represent, what were its qualities, what did it tell him about himself? For him it represented freedom, the ability to travel in difficult
terrain, ruggedness, all-weather ability – all good qualities he sought
to nurture in himself.

Retrieving a power animal is like plugging back into a power source. At times in our life when we get dispirited and down, we tend to be susceptible to illness. From a shamanic point of view, we have lost power. These are times when we can be subject to accidents or what appears like 'bad luck' (although there is no such thing!) These are indications that all is not well and we are power-less and it is time to take a journey to reconnect and restore power.

In the old cultures the shaman would do the journeying while the apprentice or helper drummed. In today's world it feels appropriate for each of us to learn to journey for ourselves and restore our own power, and in workshops that is what we teach first. However, once one is familiar with one's own lower and upperworlds, it is very revealing and informative to journey in pairs for each other. Soul retrieval (*see later in this chapter*) is much better done for someone else.

There are many books with classifications of meanings of power animals such as the excellent *Medicine Cards* by Jamie Sams. However, when you journey it is *your* psyche that throws up the image and so the first question to be pondered is 'What does it represent to me?' When journeying in the lowerworld there is one great source of information – the animal itself! When in doubt ask your animal.

The next journey to do after retrieving your power animal and becoming familiar with it, is a journey to ask a major life question. Just one question per journey, and it is important to get it really clear. Power animals, in my experience, do not like messy questions and will express disgust unless one goes to them having done one's own share of the work!

The following examples of journeys come from the files of my colleague Howard Charing. Howard came to shamanism via a near death experience in a lift crash some 15 years ago which left him severely injured, unable to stand or walk. This accident made him severely depressed and lacking the will to live. He told me: 'Healing began when I made the *decision* to get better.' As time went by he found himself in touch with other realities and wondered if he was going off the wall. He found he was able to help other people by travelling to non-ordinary places where he would come across an aspect of the person which was in danger, or bound up in some way and so on. Along the way he encountered animals who were clearly there to assist him in the exploration and healing work.

We met about six years ago at a sweatlodge ceremony I was running for a small group of friends. Up till then he had not known of such a thing as 'shamanism', and it was when introduced to the ways of the shamans and the methodology of the classic shamanic journey that he realized that that was what he had been spontaneously doing. In his own words: 'I found that all the things I was doing were validated by ancient shamanic practices. The discipline of shamanism enabled me to stop thinking I was off the wall and to be able to enter and return from altered states at will.' In a vision he saw an Indian brave who beckoned him down into a dark lodge lit just by the glow of the sacred pipe. The old Indian told him his work was to teach the old ways in a new way.

The following examples of journeys come from Howard's client files. The first describes an exploratory journey:

*I looked around and everywhere had a blue tint.*
*I felt very warm and comfortable, then I saw*
*some animals appear from out of the trees. I was*

*surprised by the detail and clarity. There was a
horse, and a moose which came very close to me
and sat down. The moose just looked at me in a
friendly yet detached way. Shortly after this a
gorilla came along carrying a drum, and then
started to beat it. This was interesting as it was
distinct from yet not discordant with the drum
being played in ordinary reality. Then a bear
appeared and stood still for a while before turning
back into the woods. As soon as that occurred,
the call-back on the drum sounded, and I started
my return.*

The next participant found certain parts of her journey difficult, but
she found the overall experience very rewarding and enhancing.

*I started off in my own garden, where there is a
small rabbit burrow, and just before I entered the
burrow a snake appeared. It had a furry, cat-like
head and I felt it to be very supportive and
friendly. We both went into the burrow where we
moved down a twisting tunnel and eventually
(it seemed to take a long time) came into a cave.
I felt very relaxed with the cat-snake. The cave
was filled with crystals, they were everywhere –
on the walls, hanging down from the roof, and
standing both in clusters and singly on the
ground. We walked further through the crystal
cave and then I felt a sensation of fear. As I felt
this, I saw a giant black spider in the centre of an
enormous thick black web in the passage in front
of us. I asked it to go, which it did, and scurried*

*down a hole in the ground. The companion snake
kind of melted the web, and we walked through.
Shortly after this, we came to a place which I knew
to be doubt. This was a broken stone bridge over a
deep chasm. The companion snake stretched itself
over the chasm and became a link to the other side.
Although I felt a bit scared, I had just enough
confidence to tiptoe gently on the 'bridge'. I did
stumble but I managed to keep my balance and
once on the other side I felt drawn to what seemed
to be a chamber. We entered the chamber, and in
the centre of the chamber was a shining bright
blue quartz crystal on a stone rectangular altar.*

*I picked up the quartz crystal, and as I did this,
I felt it being absorbed , melting into my heart
– I really felt this physically! It was a beautiful
warming sensation, and then the call-back
sounded and I started my return with the snake.
What an amazing experience!*

This journey illustrates the motifs of the downwards tunnel, and
even though the journeyer had not yet intended to connect to a
power animal it was clear that a power animal had wanted to be
with her. She intuitively felt that the power animal was helping and
supporting her, and she correctly gauged the friendly feelings that
the animal had for her.

Here is a journey which shows how a power animal can guide and
inform during a journey. The journeyer was a man who had suffered
serious injuries to his legs in an accident. There was no specific
intention for the journey, except to be with the power animal.

*I moved into the entrance which was a cave.*
*I found a hole, and started to climb down on a*
*ladder. This seemed to go on for ever, and I felt*
*that it would just take too long, so I jumped*
*down, and fell down and down. I landed in a cave,*
*and it felt as if my legs had been damaged in*
*the fall, I couldn't even feel my legs, I couldn't*
*support myself, or get up. My legs had withered*
*and twisted in a most contorted way.*

*My power animal was there in the cave; it lifted*
*me up and gave me a piggyback ride. There was*
*just no way I could walk. We moved out into*
*the open, the light was unusual, it was a bright*
*green. In the distance I could see what appeared*
*to be a city, yet it was different from any other*
*city, the buildings looked like saucers and domes.*
*Anyway the power animal set off in this*
*direction. It moved down into a valley where*
*the city was, everything was round and curved.*
*The colours were metallic: green, crimson, blue,*
*they all had this anodized metallic coloured*
*appearance. We moved in the streets of the city,*
*there were some people walking around, there*
*was also a mix of animal-drawn carts, and*
*vehicles which silently hovered. The power animal*
*took me to a place which I recognized as some*
*kind of medical centre; we went in, and I was laid*
*on a table. A machine was placed over the lower*
*half of my body and my legs started to repair –*
*the legs untwisted, and became strong and full*
*again. I felt in my physical body that I was being*

*stretched out, and my pelvic area was being forced back. I felt much flatter. My knees were also examined by this device. I felt lots of tightness and tension in my knees, and my body felt much stronger. When it was over, I was keen to start exploring this place. I stood up and found that my legs were strong again. I said thank you to the medical people, who were humans, wearing white and were smiling at me. We moved on, and we both ran out of the city and up the hill. This was an exhilarating experience.*

It was interesting to note that the journeyer did experience a simultaneous change in the physical world as the healing work was being carried out in non-ordinary reality. He reported that he really did feel a change, and that his legs did feel stronger, and that he no longer felt so twisted. This is a clear example where the spirits did have mercy on this person and were able to help.

# *The Upperworld*

A typical journey to the upperworld you may be familiar with is the psychosynthesis guided visualization up a mountain to visit a 'Wise Person' who lives at the top. Other typical journeys are by climbing a magic tree which goes miles up into the sky, or by being lifted up by whirlwind or tornado, or by climbing the Axis Mundi, the world tree. Many fairy-tales and legends speak of this, such as Jack and the Beanstalk, although the giant Jack encounters is more of a typical lowerworld image. As with the lowerworld, the shaman can journey to the upperworld to find help and guidance, though not to 'retrieve' a guide!

In many Western traditions a great split has occurred between concepts of the upper and lower worlds. For example, in the Judao-Christian tradition they have become heaven and hell and in the Greek tradition Mount Olympus where the good gods reside and Hades where the baddies are. This split is part of the split I talked about in Chapter 2 which so desperately calls out for healing in our collective Western psyche. While all the 'good' gods are in the sky realm and all the 'bad' ones down on earth in 'Hell' or 'Hades', what hope is there for us to value and love the earth? Hell originally meant light and comes from the Greek *Helles*. Helen is the goddess of light. And the Native American goddess Wyola-Helle, goddess of the prairie, is known as Prairie-Light.

Interestingly, in Siberian mythology the creator gods live in the upperworld but show little interest in the affairs of humans, while the gods who created earth live in the lowerworld, show great interest and concern for the affairs of humans and can be called on for help by shamans – which is a rather more earth-friendly mythology!

## *Soul Retrieval*

Most, if not all of us have experienced soul loss. It certainly happened to me with traumas such as being sent away to boarding school at the age of eight, which I experienced as abandonment. What made it so difficult was that it was abandonment 'because we love you'. If that's love, give me less of it! I also experienced it around puberty when the family structure, such as it was, disintegrated for a time. At the same time I was at the boarding school I detested and I remember how I went into 'survival mode' just to get through, squashed a chunk of my aliveness and did my best to feel as little as possible.

Typically we experience soul loss as a result of a severe trauma. A part of our vital nature goes into hiding so that we can survive what is happening. So in a time of extreme stress, in order for the whole self to survive, a fragment of the soul leaves. This is a natural survival mechanism which helps at the time but then needs attention in later life if we want to become whole again.

Symptoms of soul loss are such things as an inability to get your life to work, inability to focus and concentrate, a lack of connection to your emotional body, a feeling of being 'spaced out' and not really present, a feeling of being an observer in the drama of your life rather than a participant; depression; an all pervasive feeling of fear. Chronic illness, especially repetitive bad health, can indicate soul loss and I think that some recently diagnosed illnesses such as ME are related to this.

In the shamanic world view, the ability to maintain good health is a matter of power. If the body is power-full (meaning power over one's self rather than manipulative power over others), there is no room for disease and illness, which are seen as invasive forces, to enter.

In the shamanic way of seeing the world, there is no such thing as linear time. You saw on the medicine wheel (*Chapter 3*) that the body exists in the present (the west). Emotions are about the past, and the mind plans the future, but the body exists only now. Memory is stored in the body, so whatever happened in the past is, in that sense, still happening somewhere. The shaman can therefore journey to that place, find out what happened, and bring back the fragment of lost soul and the life force it contains.

# The Soul Retrieval Journey

The journey for soul retrieval is similar to the power animal journey described earlier. It involves going down the tunnel to the lowerworld, connecting with one's power animal and any other helpers one may develop as one gains experience, and then journeying to the lower-world of the client. Sometimes a side tunnel will appear off one's own tunnel which will lead directly there. The power animal or helper will then lead one to the place where the soul fragment is. The fragment, which is often in a state of distress, appears usually as a younger version of the client, and may not be at all happy to come back, so that a negotiation may have to take place to prove it is now safe to return. It is then a case of bringing back the soul part and blowing the life force back into the client. This creates an energy change which takes from three days to about two weeks to fully integrate, and the person may well need therapy or some form of support while the change is taking place. The soul fragment departed for a good reason, it is not going to stay around if those reasons are still present.

Soul retrieval is therapeutic but it is not therapy. However, it is a great help at times, such as when the therapeutic process is stalled, and it can bring a magical change to a person's inner energy. It is good to have support after soul retrieval so one doesn't miss the great opportunity of having that life-force returned, but uses it.

A therapist can only work with the parts of a person which are actually there! Soul retrieval can bring missing parts back and hence facilitate the therapeutic process. As a specialist in soul retrieval, Howard tells me he is finding some people are now coming to sessions accompanied by their therapist, which he feels is a highly encouraging development.

Buried memories and emotions, often uncomfortable, will resurface after soul retrieval. This is a sign that healing is taking place. In all deep level healing things get worse before they get better! The pus in the wound must come out fully before the wound heals or full healing cannot take place.

At one of our residential workshops Howard did a demonstration soul retrieval for a participant. We will call him Martin. I drummed for him, quietly so he could recount the journey for everyone to hear. He entered Martin's lowerworld quite easily, but the journey was long and difficult and my drumming hand had nearly fallen off by the end!

On return he blew the retrieved part back by blowing through his cupped hands at Martin's heart area. It is the intention that matters here, the blowing is just a vehicle for the intention. There was no immediate change in Martin whatsoever. He was a shy, quiet, retiring person, almost grey in a sense. It was much later in the workshop – about three days – that in a sharing circle we suddenly saw a very different Martin as he shared deeply about himself and his life with an energy that belied any previous sense of greyness.

I am handing over the rest of this chapter to Howard. Here are some very interesting examples of soul retrieval. All names and places have been changed

## *Soul Retrieval Journeys*

Nicole came to see me complaining about a pervasive feeling of being threatened. She felt that it was something 'within' her, yet was unable to get a handle on this. She felt uneasy and distrustful, and pleasure in her family and work had become difficult. Nicole is a practising health care professional, divorced with two children, and in her mid-thirties. I discussed this with her, and she confirmed that there were events happening around her where she felt threatened and in danger. We discussed the shamanic journey, and agreed that we would start off with no preconceived ideas.

*We both lay down on my special Journey rug, with our elbows and shoulders touching. I find it helpful to have this contact, as in some way it is a physical confirmation that we are on this journey together. I placed the earphones and started the drumming tape, and as the sound started I found myself moving into my entrance into the lower-world, and then swiftly moving down and down. I then found myself near a spiral staircase, and I knew that I was now moving into Nicole's personal map of the lowerworld. I walked, and sometimes ran, very deep down this spiral staircase. At times I found myself becoming slightly giddy with this, and occasionally took a brief pause. After what felt like a long time I came to a building that had the appearance of a prison – there was a high wall, and all the windows and doors had bars. Awaiting me was a representation of Nicole, she beckoned me to follow, and as I did this, she led me into a prison cell and locked the door to trap me.*

*This was an attempt to stop any further exploration, a form of defence using trickery and deception. I spoke out aloud to Nicole, I told her*

*what had happened, and asked her if it was okay*
*to continue. She was anxious for the journey to*
*go on. I then melted the bars and escaped out of*
*the prison.*

(Just a note here. In the lowerworld people often have a degree of power over matter and can influence the landscape. It is easier when this journey is done on behalf of another person, as there is no personal involvement with the inner landscape.)

*When I had got out, the image of Nicole*
*transformed into a giant. I was able to reverse the*
*transformation and reduce the giant in size.*
*When this happened, a young girl aged about two*
*years appeared looking extremely frightened.*
*I spent some time with the child giving her*
*reassurance and comfort. I asked her what she*
*needed, and although she could not speak out, it*
*was clear that she sought to be loved and cared*
*for by her adult self. It was at this point that one*
*of my spirit guides arrived. This spirit guide*
*appears to me as a Tibetan lama wearing*
*beautiful red and saffron clothes, his face exudes*
*kindness, love, and above all a simple gentleness.*
*He explained that Nicole had fallen down a steep*
*hill at that age, felt great fear and had gone into*
*shock. He showed me an image of how this*
*happened, which I relayed to Nicole. I felt her*
*body shudder as she remembered this incident.*
*The spirit guide indicated that he would stay with*
*the young girl whilst I continued on the journey.*
*He reached out to hold the little girl's hand, I saw*

*her face relax and become gentle. Even though I
hadn't yet relayed this event to Nicole, it was
interesting to get confirmation of this as I felt
her body immediately relax and her breath
became slower.*

*I moved outside the prison area. Surrounding it
was a dark, deep sea. I went in, it felt cold and
heavy. I continued to swim until I saw a small
island onto which I climbed. The land was very
wobbly and appeared to be just floating on the
surface of the sea rather than being connected to
the ground. As I looked around me, there were
many pieces and clumps of land floating on the
surface. On the island that I was standing on was
a serpent. I went to the serpent and asked why it
was here. The serpent described itself as the
envies of others who had or were in love. I told
Nicole this and she confirmed this trait in herself.
She agreed that it was time to release this as it
was neither needed or helpful. As she did this in
the physical world I worked with the serpent, to
transmute it into something more appropriate.
The serpent changed into a coloured rainbow-like
light and disappeared.*

*I then asked my spirit helpers for guidance as
to what to do next. I saw an image of all the
separate floating clumps of land coming together,
joining. I started to do this slowly, piece by piece
bringing each small island together and fusing
them into one. I started from the sea bed, and*

105

reconstructed the land mass from the bottom upwards. When this was complete a snarling, angry, savage beast attacked me. I was able to keep it at arm's length. I asked Nicole to connect to this. She immediately responded with 'self-sabotage'. I was able to encourage the beast to change and it burst into flames, and as the carcass burned there stood within the inner-being a young girl called Hannah. Nicole identified Hannah with a past life experience in a concentration camp. This initiated a powerful emotional release and a reluctance to work with Hannah.

It was time to start on the journey back and I held Hannah's hand as we did this. The landscape had totally changed, it really was a 'new land'. Life was returning, plants were growing, there was the sound of birds, the smell of rich earth and the scent of flowers around. As we walked through this beautiful country we came to a tree of massive dimensions. This tree had deep roots into the earth and many branches filled with leaves. I felt strongly that the tree acted as a binding force holding this new land together. The tree looked strong and abundant.

It was quite a joyful surprise when I saw the lama spirit guide with the two-year old girl sitting there waiting for us. I spoke to Nicole, and told her what had happened and where we were, and it was then that she decided that she did want to *be with the child Hannah. I felt this to be very satisfactory, and the lama nodded in approval. We moved onwards to the entrance back to our world. The lama spirit waved farewell to us and I, with both children in my arms, started the ascent upwards.*

*I returned with the children and with a small ceremony brought them both back to be with Nicole.*

*Nicole's immediate response was that she felt energized, clearer, and just lighter in her body. I spoke with her a week or so later and she said that that night she had gone to bed early and had the best night's sleep for ages. The following days she had felt joyful, yet this was tinged with sadness as some of the emotions relating to the experiences in the journey worked through her being. It took about four to five days until she really felt good about herself. She was delighted to have this reflected back from people around her who said that she looking radiant. I asked her if she still had the feeling of being threatened. Her response was no, the world feels a better place now: 'I have a sense of more expansiveness. I know it was all me, but I was seeing it as if it was from outside of me.'*

One of the aspects of journeying into the other realities is encountering events that occurred long ago and may have been forgotten or suppressed by our conscious mind. In a sense they can be seen to be still taking place if the event is still affecting us. These I classify as 'secrets', my definition being that the individual is not consciously aware of these events, yet 'what happened' as a result of these events is still operating and having its effect.

I would like to illustrate this with another example:

> Margaret, a person in her late twenties, always had, as far as she could remember, a sense of being smothered. Even though she knew that this was not logical (she displayed a finely detailed analytical approach to her life), and that there was no reason for this, it still affected her and made her fearful.

> We lay down next to each other, put the drumming tape on, and started the journey down into the lowerworld. I went deep down and I came into a nocturnal forest. My power animal was waiting for me, and after we greeted each other, I asked how I could best help Margaret. My power animal responded by indicating that I should follow him. We ran through the night landscape and into a forest; it was completely dark. I felt okay moving through this land, as I had confidence in the power animal who clearly knew where to go. We came into a clearing; I sensed space around us, a breeze, and I was aware of the night sky above even though there were no stars.

> In this clearing I gradually became aware that Margaret was there, she was hurt and crying.

*I asked my power animal what had happened and*
*I saw a scene where Margaret was attacked and*
*raped. The rapist threatened her with a knife, and*
*although Margaret didn't see it, she did not resist.*
*This appeared to be a safe choice because it was*
*very clear that the assailant was prepared to use*
*this knife.*

*After this scene the power animal indicated that*
*I should follow him. I held the hand of Margaret*
*and we all entered a cave. It was even darker here*
*than outside, the blackness was total and I could*
*feel the fear of being smothered very powerfully.*
*I asked the power animal what this cave was.*
*He said the heart was like a black cavern to*
*Margaret, a lot of self-destructive, almost*
*suicidal energy was here and needed clearing.*
*This self-destructive energy appeared; it had the*
*form and shape of an octopus, the body and*
*tentacles were heavy and black. Both the power*
*animal and I had to work to change the density*
*of this form, to enable it to be released.*

*Margaret, who was listening to my simultaneous*
*narration of this journey, said that after the rape*
*she had been going to throw herself under the*
*wheels of a train. She then started to release*
*much of her sorrow, emotions that she later said*
*she had cut herself off from.*

*After this, a soft light appeared in the cave and*
*another scene played. We found out that her*

mother had also been raped and that the source
of her fear of being smothered was when she was
thrown into her cot by her mother at the time of
the assault. Margaret realized that she had picked
up on her mother's fears and in some way had
replayed them in her life.

The cave became lighter and we all exited into the
open air. Outside the sun was starting to rise and
we could see the forest. The air became warm,
it was a very pleasant day and the three of us
walked back into the forest towards the entrance.
On the way, we stopped at a clear lake where the
soul part of Margaret bathed and cleansed herself.
At the entrance I said farewell to my power
animal and brought back the soul part to
ordinary reality.

We carried out the returning ceremony. Margaret
just felt a great relief, her body just let out this
great big sigh, and she visibly relaxed.

She called me a couple of weeks later to tell me
that her life was starting to change. She felt she
was able to trust, to follow her feelings and
instincts. She said that there had been a
noticeable shift within her and she no longer felt
that she needed to control people and events in
the way and to the extent that she used to. I
received another call from her a couple of months
later, and she said that life was really opening up
for her – things were great!

In the following soul retrieval journey, the recipient has written to me in his own words. While on a field visit to Peru, the man had suffered serious injuries in a road accident. I often hear from people who after an accident or major surgery say that 'they haven't felt the same since then'. His story, which clearly illustrates this, follows:

> *I had been involved in a road accident five months previously which had left me with a badly broken leg. I was in an awful state of depression, lacking energy and vitality. I could only describe it as feeling that I was 'not here', that I was either drugged or asleep. I felt half-dead to the world, really unable to function effectively or with any enthusiasm. During the soul retrieval session it was explained to me that a large part of my life-force had left at the time of the accident and was still there at the scene in a state of shock. A road scene was described which matched the actual place. I realized that it was true, and that I wasn't here – I was three thousand miles away in Peru!*

> *Within minutes of the soul retrieval, when my lost soul parts were being blown back into me, I felt alive again for the first time in five months. The effect was so dramatic – enthusiasm, vitality, energy and joy returned. It was like something that I had never experienced before.*

> *It's been some weeks now since the soul retrieval and I can say it's been the most extraordinarily therapeutic experience I have ever had. I feel that I am 'here' again, back home.*

The final soul retrieval journey shows how decisions we have made in the past and have forgotten still affect our present lives.

*Francesca, a woman in her late 30s, came to see me. She said that she always felt 'spaced-out' and not 'in' her body. She was confused by this, as she was sure that she had not had any trauma in her life and could not understand where these feelings came from. She added that she always felt tired and low on energy. Her sex life was near non-existent, even though she had a lengthy relationship with her partner. I felt that the best thing to do would be to make a journey to the other realities, where I would ask the teachers and spirit guides what needed to be done.*

*We lay next to each other and I started the drumming tape. My initial intention was to make a brief exploratory journey to find out what needed to be done. Francesca was already interested in shamanism, so the terminology and the concepts of what I was doing were quite familiar to her. I journeyed down into the lower-world; my power animal was waiting for me there. I asked him for his help and he showed me an image of Francesca's body. On this image, the stomach area was black and there were circular shadows on her body which, on zooming in, were revealed to be hooks into her body. My power animal then indicated for me to follow him. We were going to a place where I had recently been. I recognized the landscape – more interestingly,*

*I was walking along the same path and the grass
was still crumpled from a previous journey. As we
were walking my power animal stopped and
produced a large mirror. I looked in the mirror
and could see reflected in it two animals, one was
a wolf and the other was a fox. This didn't have
any meaning for me and I couldn't quite
understand what the relevance was. I was
simultaneously narrating this out aloud so
Francesca would be aware of what was
happening, and also of my confusion. We
continued further and we came to a tree house
where I knew one of my guides (in human form)
lived. We climbed up there and he was waiting. He
told me that Francesca would need two soul
retrievals and work in the middleworld to remove
and extract some intrusions. I thanked him for
the information and started to make my way
back – the initial objective to gather information
had been met.*

*I returned to this reality and reviewed the
elements of the journey with Francesca. She
confirmed that she had an unpleasant pain in her
stomach and it was too sensitive even to touch.
When I had mentioned the hooks in her body, she
knew what the source of these was. Francesca
explained that she had joined a psychic
development group where the leader had
started to develop a large ego and was
abusing her position.*

*Francesca observed that this leader was*
*controlling and manipulating the group in a way*
*that disempowered it. When she spoke up against*
*what was going on, she was made to feel very*
*uncomfortable, even humiliated by this leader. I*
*realized that this was the work that my guide had*
*said would need to be done in the middleworld.*
*I asked about the animals and she said that they*
*were her power animals. I asked her if she ever*
*visited them, she said very rarely. I suggested*
*that she should, as they obviously wanted to*
*communicate with her.*

The rest of this session focused on removing the psychic hooks put in place by the group leader and doing extraction healing work on her stomach area.

We met again a week later. Francesca said that she felt stronger, that her capacity for reasoning was returning and that other people had noticed a change in her. She was becoming more active and sleeping less (before she had been oversleeping). Here are my notes from the first Soul Retrieval:

*We lay down together, I started the drumming*
*tape and gently relaxed as I moved into the*
*shamanic state of consciousness. I moved down*
*and down, deep down, and I came into her map*
*of the lowerworld. I was happy to see my power*
*animal waiting there for me. The place was like*
*a barren land, no apparent life, no vegetation.*
*There were great rifts in the land. I didn't know*
*where to go in this place, and as I thought this*

*another of my guides appeared. This guide has the appearance of an Aborigine tracker. My experience is that he can track anything, yet when he does appear I know that it will be a long and arduous journey, that his skills are not loaned to me without a reason. My feelings were confirmed when my power animal did not want to accompany us, but preferred to wait for us. We took our farewell, the tracker moved off and I followed him. The land became increasingly desolate and barren – the total sensation of barrenness started to become overpowering, there was just nothing around. I even felt that the tracker spirit was not too sure of which direction to go and what exactly we were looking for. It was then that I saw a bird, which I knew to be a raven, flying high. The tracker guide and I started to follow the bird. The bird had a feel of death around it. We saw that the raven flew into a nest located in a cave entrance high up on a sheer rock face.*

*We climbed up the rock face and entered into the cave where the nest was. Looking in the nest we saw an entrance leading down into another, even deeper level of the lowerworld. We moved in and found ourselves in a grim corridor. Ahead of us was a dense mist which I understood to be a way into the 'land of the dead'. We entered the mist, it was difficult to find our way or even move. I held the hand of the tracker spirit and followed him. We finally came out of the mist and found*

*ourselves to be in another rocky barren
landscape. However this time there was a small
round dwelling ahead. We entered the hut and
inside was Francesca, looking downtrodden and
in complete thrall to another woman, much older
than her. At that moment, another of my guides
came in (the one whom we had visited in our
previous journey). He told me that the woman
that Francesca was in thrall to was herself, and
that she should return with us while the elder
woman should stay.*

*We started the return journey, back into the mist,
and we retraced our path until finally we came
to the entrance where my power animal was
waiting. I said my farewell to the tracker spirit
and brought Francesca's soul part back with me.
Francesca released a lot of emotion and tears, she
said that she had made a decision to go away to
protect herself from years of abuse.*

The following week we did the second soul retrieval:

*At first Francesca spoke about her feelings and
what had come up for her the past week. She said
that she had been crying a lot, having tantrums,
feeling depressed, suicidal, hating herself and all
that goes with that. I listened carefully to what
she was saying. She was now experiencing
feelings from which she had previously cut herself
off. She was now more alive and a part of our life
as humans is to have feelings: this was what was*

*happening. My heart went out to her and I told
her that she had been extremely courageous with
this. She wanted to know why she could not
receive, what was stopping this?*

*I started the journey and the tunnel downwards
became a slide. Then the downwards tunnel
became blocked and it did not appear possible to
descend further. As I landed on the blockage, my
power animal was there and he indicated a side
tunnel. Rubble filled this tunnel, we were able to
make a path through this and come out into a
landscape. This landscape was frozen, very cold,
with icy winds howling, all looked to be grey. We
moved out into this place and listened to the
sound of snow crunching beneath our feet. On an
incline was a ram and I asked the animal the
question that Francesca wanted to ask, 'Why can
she not receive?'. The answer from the ram was
that, 'She believes that she will freeze to death
and die.' I asked for more information and
received an image of Francesca ensconced in ice.
Where was this? The ram indicated with its hoof
and head downwards and then he knocked a hole
through the ice. Below the ice was a chamber. We
climbed into this chamber and found it to be like
an ancient Egyptian antechamber. It was filled
with artefacts, statues, furniture, mummy cases.
There was another door that led off, I opened it
and went in. This room was extremely cold, I
really felt cold, not only in the journey but also in
my physical body in normal reality. In this room*

*the walls were ice. I started to thaw them and the
ram joined us at that moment. We saw the soul
part of Francesca in the ice, and focused our
warmth and heat onto that area. We saw lots of
imagery of Francesca as a baby, not getting any
love, not receiving warmth, and being bound very
tightly. The ice had melted, I reached out and took
her by the hand, the whole place was starting to
thaw, to warm up. As we climbed out of the
chamber the landscape was melting, the ice and
snow were turning into slush, the sun was out,
shining warmth. We saw a flock of birds fly
in formation above our heads and we knew
everything would be okay.*

*We returned the way that we came. Francesca
was excited by this journey and what had
happened. 'I can feel my body! My chest has
warmth! My shoulders! I feel much younger and
lighter!' She looked a lot softer, she understood
that her problems were not about receiving, but
about being frozen, and as she looked at her
clothes which were coloured icy grey she laughed.
The irony was not lost on her. Her final comment
was 'No longer the ice maiden!'*

# DANCE AND TRANCE-DANCE

## A Gateway to Healing

*If I Can Talk I Can Sing, If I Can Walk I Can Dance!*

AFRICAN SAYING

This saying doesn't mention anything about being good enough or singing 'in tune' or getting anything right! Our ancestors all over the planet sang and danced to connect with spirit, to heal and balance themselves and to celebrate. From Africa to America to India and the Far East, to Europe and to Australia, people have sung and danced. Think of the incredible dancing and drum rhythms of West Africa, the whirling of the Persian Dervishes, the magnificent costumed dances of the Native Americans, the masked dancers of Bali, the Candomble and Umbanda trance-dancers of Brazil, the Gnawas of Morocco, Tai Chi, the dancing martial art of the far east, the Eskimo, the Sioux, the Huichols of the Sierra Madre in Mexico, and so on and on. Dancing is a primal way to reach altered states of consciousness, to reach out of the confines of the everyday trance and to touch the liminal. Dancing helps us return fully into our body and take our body to Spirit.

The way of the shaman says we are spirits learning how to live in a body given by Mother Earth. That's why we are here – to learn to live in a body – and to bring the whole of ourselves, body, mind, emotions and spirit into harmony and balance. We are not in a body to get out of it and escape by becoming 'spiritual' or religious; we are here to learn how to be in matter, and how to bring matter and spirit together. Dancing is just the greatest way to do that and has been part of human culture for probably 40 – 50,000 years, perhaps much longer.

# Dance Warm-ups

It is absolutely essential to prepare the ground before attempting to enter a trance dance. The first thing is to perform stretches and gentle warming up of the musculature and joints. This avoids the pain of pulled muscles. Then a series of short partnered dances can help one to leave behind whatever has been going on in the day and come nearer to the here and now. Some exercises I often use in Shamanic Dance sessions go like this:

## Dance the four directions

Take an *animal totem* for each direction (*see map of the Four Directions in Chapter 3*), such as serpent for the south, jaguar for the west, horse for the north and eagle for the east. Those are typical Inca totems. With suitable music, dance each one for about five to ten minutes while calling that energy to be with you and dance through you.

## Dance the four elements

Dance water (South), earth (West), wind, (North) and fire (East). Again, choose a suitable drumbeat or other music, and dance each one, calling the feeling of the element to be with you and dance through you.

Dance the *qualities* of the directions and even the battle between them and their enemies. That makes a very interesting dance and goes like this: Dance fear versus trust (South), inertia versus introspection (West), clarity (know-all-ness) versus wisdom (North), and (misuse of) power versus illumination/ enlightenment (East). Again, choose suitable rhythms and dance each for maybe five to ten minutes, or however long the energy of the group sustains it. It is easy to make up dances like this from the medicine wheels of the directions in chapter three.

## *Sound Into Movement*

Bring the group together in the centre of the room and start a long note, adding harmonies and expressions to it until it is a free expression of the group voice. Then fade in the drums or the music and gradually let the spirit of dance take over. I find this works best in a candlelit room. It can go on for quite a long time and take the people deeper than one might expect.

## *Finding the Rhythm Within*

When everyone is dancing their own dance without a partner, slowly fade the music to silence while exhorting the group to continue the dance and find their own inner rhythms. It is interesting to then get them to interchange with a series of partners, and after that to change partners quickly and repeatedly until they just interact and move on. The room can feel like one pulsing energy when everyone 'touches' everyone momentarily and allows each other's movement to affect them. Then slowly fade the music back in.

## *Blind Dance*

This is a good practice to do before trance-dancing because it helps one to have confidence while dancing with eyes closed. Everyone partners up. One of the partners becomes the guide and the other closes their eyes and dances blind while protected by their partner. It is best for the partners to hold one or both hands, certainly to start with, and for the guide to guide the blind partner and swing them around.

# Gabrielle Roth's Wave Dance of the Five Rhythms

Gabrielle calls her form of dance *The Wave*. The first movement is *flowing* – watery, easy, yet purposeful; feminine, yielding but not weak. Add more strength and definite purpose and you gradually move into *staccato*, the second movement, which is masculine, demanding, purposeful, strong and forceful. Let this become more and more so until a moment is reached when the energy can no longer be contained and it naturally bursts forth into *chaos*, the third segment where all is wild movement. This goes on as long as the energy is there and then gradually subsides into *lyrical*: light and relaxing, coming down, the moment after, when one is almost out-of-body, flowing again yet with such ease as to be the flow, the dance moving the dancer, the energy unrestricted, the body loose and a smile on your face. Then everything slows down to *stillness,* the last movement, feeling the life force, existence, 'beingness' – nothing and everything all at once.

*The Wave* is the orgasm cycle too. The *flowing* is like foreplay, teasing the energy out of hiding, stoking the fires, raising the winds of libido; then the energy demands to express itself and the *staccato* motion affirms and takes over, raising the energy toward the inevitability of *chaos* up and up, faster and faster, demanding its expression, until the orgasm happens and glorious chaos reigns. A good long *chaos* dance is like a multi-orgasm in motion. Then the *lyrical,* coming down, slowly and easily, the time of no-time, when the body has emptied and made room for the Spirit, and the dance dances the dancer, the spirit moves within, until stillness of healthy exhaustion takes over and the heartbeat of existence is all that is left.

Gabrielle's excellent book *Maps to Ecstasy* covers her work.

## Native American style LongDance

This is quite literally a long dance! It can be all night – as night-time is the best time to shut down normal senses and open up to the subtle realms – or a short LongDance can be an evening for about four hours. The essence of a LongDance is to dance and dance and dance around and around in a sunwise circle, usually around a fire, with drummers supporting and putting their energy into creating a sacred space where one can reach into that magic where the dance dances the dancer until, perhaps, the dancer disappears into the dance.

The power of the LongDance is shown by the following magical event. This happened over 10 years ago at one of my New Year workshops at Grimstone Manor in Devon, where my friend Kenneth Meadows experienced a shamanic journey. He was shown a lantern whose light would enable people of all cultures and traditions to find their own inner beauty and path to fulfilment. This lantern now shines brightly in the form of five books, *Earth Medicine, The Medicine Way, Shamanic Experience, Where Eagles Fly*, and *Rune Power* (Element Books).

Kenneth described to me something of his experience which he said extended over three to four hours:

> *The experience I had was of alternating between the 'ordinary' reality of dancing around a fire to constant drumming and rattling, and a 'non-ordinary' reality which was just as real. During the periods of ordinary awareness I broke off from the dancing to make notes of what I had experienced in this other state of awareness. (I remember thinking at the time that I must have made a mess of my instructions about the ceremony because it was not supposed to include writing!) It was not until later that I recognized that much of this writing was in poetic form though I had not previously written poetry or even attempted it.*
>
> *There was also a fire in this parallel reality into which the 'dancers' cast what they were carrying. I was 'told', not in audible words but intuitively, that what was being offered to the flames were sacred teachings which could only be reclaimed from the fire of the spirit. I was invited to pick up a stick and light it from the flames so that it became a torch. The torch was to be used to light a lantern which I was to make.*
>
> *It seemed to me that the components of the lantern were to be books which I must write. On reflection afterwards that seemed an utter impossibility. My knowledge of shamanism at*

*that time was very limited. I considered I would
be hard pressed to write a short article, let alone
a book. Later I was given an assurance that both
the teachers and teachings to enable this would
come to me at the appropriate times.*

*For more than 10 years from the time I went
home and began to write, this has been a literal
fact in my life. As a result I have written in excess
of half a million published words. And this is
still ongoing, having survived my near death
experience and open-heart surgery – and there
is much yet to be written.*

*Much of the poetic words written from the Long
Dance experience contained concepts which made
little sense to me at the time. Understanding has
developed gradually through the years as the
work of constructing the 'lantern' has progressed
and the purpose of that experience has become
manifest.*

## *Power Animal Dance*

This is a way to exercise one's connection with a power animal.

Standing in a circle with other people, make your hands into fists
and begin to move them up and down together in rhythm to a
steady walking-pace drumbeat or rattle. Then add to this by stomp-
ing left-right-left with your feet. After maybe two to three minutes,
turn to your left and begin to move around in a circle calling your

power animal to dance through you. As this begins to happen, break the circle form and let your own dance manifest and with it the sounds of your animal. The drummers speed up the beat and flow with the energy of the dancers until you find yourselves in the jungle! The dance continues as long as the energy is there for it. Then rest and share with a partner what you experienced.

If you are alone you can do this dance by rattling for yourself, though it is much better done in a group. This dance can help reacquaint us with the wild wo/man within. In the words of Michael Harner from *The Way Of The Shaman:* (Bantam Books) 'One thing that usually becomes clear to the dancers is that underneath our ordinary human cultural consciousness is a near-universal emotional connection with wild animal alter egos.'

# *Firebreath*

This is not a dance but it belongs here as it is a way into altered states and can be used to precede a trance dance.

Lie on the floor with your knees up and feet flat. Breathe through the mouth into the abdomen, visualizing that you are breathing through the perineum at the base of the spine, the base chakra. As you do so clench the rectal-genital muscles and imagine you are bringing the air up to the second chakra, the hara, two or three fingers widths below the navel. Relax and breathe out. Repeat, keeping a connected breath, until it feels as if you really are breathing this circle. Then bring the breath further up to the third chakra in the solar plexus. Again, keep it going until it feels that it is really happening. Then bring the breath up to the heart so that you are now inhaling from the base chakra and clenching the genital/rectal muscles, then exhaling from the heart chakra and relaxing all your muscles. Keep this going for maybe fifteen to twenty minutes and then gently relax altogether.

Once you feel happy with this exercise you can breathe up further to the throat chakra, then the third eye, and lastly to the crown of your head. This aids the streaming of energy through your whole body and is a great way into a trance space on its own or as a preliminary to trance-dance.

# Trance Dance Inductions

## Shaking warm-up

To music with a really fast beat, shake your body completely in such a way that every bit of you gets moved. Breathe fast while doing this to ventilate yourself thoroughly. Five to ten minutes will raise your energy and prepare you for getting into the dance.

## Spinning warm-up

Likewise, with fast music simply start to spin, keeping your eyes open but unfocused. Put your arms out and spin yourself around but keep to a speed within which you can stay balanced. The object is to practise the spin, not to enter a trance. Do this for about two to three minutes.

## Butterfly induction

Stand with your eyes closed, feet about shoulder width apart. Raise your arms out to the side like a butterfly opening its wings and at the same time inhale through the mouth. Lower the arms and exhale, bending the knees and sinking down a little. Start fairly slowly and increase speed gradually to your maximum and keep this going for about two or three minutes. Then let the arms slowly relax, reduce speed of breathing and begin to dance, letting it take you where it will. It is good to tie a bandanna around your eyes and to dance in the dark, allowing yourself to go deep inside.

## Breath induction

This is similar to the exercises above but is just performed with breathing. The eyes should be closed and preferably covered with a bandanna. Breathe deeply through the mouth into the abdomen and immediately exhale. Like rebirthing, the breath is 'connected' so there is no pause between either the inhale or exhale. Make sure your body feels loose, feel your feet firmly on the earth, knees slightly bent, feet shoulder width apart and parallel, shoulders, arms, hands relaxed, head hanging down from the neck and able to roll easily from side to side. Gradually speed up the breathing and continue for maybe three to five minutes until it gives you a really effective charge of energy. Then the music comes in and off you can go into the dance.

*Be careful!* High energy trance dance is not recommended for those with epilepsy or seizures, cardiovascular problems, pregnancy or severe psychotic disorders. It's just great for nice, normal, neurotics!

# Terpsichore Trance Therapy

This is the most effective induction I have experienced. Just about the most difficult thing for any Westerner to do is get out of their head, to let go of ego-control. We are like a nation of control freaks, terrified to let the Spirit enter and take us where it will. We are terrified of Spirit's Will and are forever trying to impose our own frightened little will. Whereas African traditions, along with many other old cultures, have worked with 'Spirit Possession' for centuries, we have learned to be frightened of it, largely because our religion is frightened of 'God' and has lost understanding of possession states, managing to identify them with 'evil'. So-called 'Spirit possession' is akin to ego-dispossession and that is initially a frightening phenomenon. To enter the world of spirit we have to leave behind our ego and its sense of control. If a culture says control is good (god), then it is effectively saying that ego is good. Thus to let go and let the Spirit have control becomes 'evil', an extraordinary reversal of vision.

When we let go of all that control, when we let the heart rule the head for a while, when we let the right hemisphere of the brain take over from the dominant rational left hemisphere and stop trying to work it all out, then we can allow ourselves a very different experience of Life, The Universe And Everything. Trance-dancing is a very effective tool to help us enter that space and it is also one of the oldest ways on the planet. The drum and the dance are as old as humanity.

So let us look at the experience of trance-dancing. Firstly I have found it essential to make minor adjustments to the original framework of Terpsichore Trance Therapy, or TTT. I find that to help people stay upright in the early stage of the dance, it is good to have four 'minders' surrounding the dancer instead of just one. Their task is to protect the dancer so he or she can really let go with confidence into the spirit of their dance and also do all they can to help the dancer stay upright. If by chance they do fall, then the minders can help them back into the dance as quickly as possible.

The trance dance experience has four parts, Induction, Dance, Relaxation and Integration. In a way it is like a vision quest.

## The Dance Induction

To induce the dance the dancer closes their eyes, feels the drumbeat and takes a few deep breaths. Next the leader holds their head firmly with one hand round the back – it is important to prevent bending the person's head backwards – with the other hand on their forehead. The leader then turns their head around a few times, gently at first and then gradually more strongly until the whole upper body is moving, pivoting from the waist. If possible it is good then to spin them around. A good induction is different for everyone and you have to learn by trial and error what works for different individuals. For some people a period of deep but quick panting breathing can help take them across their barriers, but I prefer to start easy and only increase the depth of induction with more experienced dancers.

## The Dance Itself

The dancers form a large circle using all the available space. One dancer comes forward to be inducted and four people are set up as minders to look after them. Once that person is off into the dance, another dancer can be inducted in another part of the room, and so on until maybe four or five, possibly even as many as six are dancing at once. This depends on the size of room and the number of participants. The drummers watch the dancers and follow where the energy is strongest. Sometimes, especially if they are playing djembes and can strap their drums on, the drummers move around

*131*

and drum right with the dancers. This is quite wonderful and it is an amazing feeling to be in the energy flow and feel oneself 'drummed' into ecstasy!

The first part of a dance is often wild and out of balance and the dancer may have difficulty staying upright. Here the minders help keep the dancer safe and do all they can to stop them actually falling down, as this can break the trance. Gradually the dance stabilises and then the trance can deepen and take the person to new vistas. After some time, fewer minders are needed until maybe just one is sufficient. Some dances go on a long time, others are higher energy and end more quickly. There is no right and wrong, it is best simply to obey the call of Spirit and let the dance dance you. The dance can take you to the upper world of light and the feeling of being beyond or outside of yourself and your usual boundaries, or it may take you to the lower world which includes repressed emotions – blocked energy – which you will usually need to clear before you can access transcendent states.

Here are the experiences of some dancers:

> *At the start I felt a huge surge of energy – as if I could take off and fly. I felt the potential for such liberation within me, and freedom of movement and expression. Simultaneously, however, as I began to dance, I felt all my limitations well up to the surface, and I experienced a real struggle inside about letting go. Something inside wouldn't let me and I felt smothered and choked by it. Before I knew it I was on the floor gasping for breath. Leo came over and said 'let it go'. I screamed out my rage; my feelings of being*

*boxed in and unable to express myself.*
*Afterwards, I felt shaken but exhilarated and with*
*a real sense of liberation.*

Then she describes her next experience:

*This time I felt a tremendous freedom and*
*liberation. I was aware and in control and yet it*
*was almost as if the outside world had been shut*
*out of my conscious mind – and even if it was*
*still there, it no longer seemed to matter. I felt*
*free and that I could do anything.*

The first dance took her into her repressed anger and frustration which needed to be released before anything else could happen. In the second dance she was free of that and so could 'fly' to the upper world and have an experience of liberation. She goes on:

*Occasionally I wondered what I must look like*
*and marvelled at how unusual it was for me to be*
*moving in the way I was – but because my focus*
*was centred within myself, what was going on*
*inside of me seemed to take priority over who or*
*what was outside of myself.*

*I was amazed afterwards how 'out of it' I was*
*– in fact it took about half an hour to feel*
*something like 'normal' again. As soon as I lay on*
*the floor I began to sob because I felt that I was*
*losing something really special in coming back*
*into my normal, limited personality and being.*
*This sadness gave way to anger as I questioned*

*why? I curled up and pondered on the way my life was. Then it dawned on me that the conditions my life seemed to impose on me were in fact of my own making – and that in fact I could be very much freer than I allowed myself to be. I began to realize with great joy that in reality there is no separation between the place I touched in the dance and my daily life. It just depends on the limitations I impose on myself.*

Another dancer writes of her first three dances. This was her first time:

*I had the feeling of being taken over. Each time the energy changed, I would fall. Although I was aware of what was going on, I could not stop or change or control the dance or the movement in any way. At the end of the dance, a few seconds before I came back I could feel waves of love moving around and through me, coming from the four directions (her four minders). It felt like when one dies and goes to that place where all the loved ones are there waiting. The love was so intense – I felt very fortunate to be dead!!!*

This was her second dance:

*I felt peaceful, could even feel a gentle smile on my face. Again I could not control or change anything. The energy was grateful to be here and was sending love and blessing to all present and lots of praise for the drummers for creating that*

*beautiful space. I felt as if I was in a far distant
place , the drums sounded so faint and far away.*

Then her third dance:

*My throat went very dry. Then suddenly it was
very dark. I thought I had become blind and was
most frightened. After a few moments, it felt like
my eyes were made of light – they were so full of
light that I found it difficult to keep them closed.
With my eyes partially open I could see the light
at the bottom of my eyes. I don't remember about
the dance. I felt wonderful.*

You can sense the development as she got accustomed to trust the
space of the dance and to let herself be fully in whatever happened.
In the third dance her psychic centres are opening a little and she is
getting a sense of her potential.

Here is another dancer's experience:

*For a long time I had felt that I had a very heavy
block in my lower abdomen and I felt as if there
were depressed emotions locked in my body. Fear
of letting them go was present but I prepared
myself to have a go.*

*After the head spinning I felt a bit panicky and
that my body was very heavy to move. After a
while I started to feel discomfort in my stomach
as I was spinning and moving. I started to feel as
if I was going to be sick. I knew all the time that*

135

*I could stop if I wanted to, but something kept me
going. It was as if something shifted inside me
and I even tasted it in my mouth, as an odour of
something old. I was holding my stomach and
continued moving. It felt slightly easier but my
body felt quite tired. I collapsed on the floor and I
was helped to bring up the cry from my stomach.
My throat felt very stiff and it was difficult to let
all the tension go.*

*After the dance I felt very quiet and slightly
shaken. Next night I slept very deep.*

Her next dance was a few weeks later:

*This time the experience was very pleasant. I felt
very free and felt that I was flying. With my eyes
closed there was a lot of light. I completely
trusted the people around me.*

*Overcoming the fear of letting go allows me to
move my conscious mind aside and tap into
another dimension which is filled with light,
colour, space and the drums. I feel as if the drum
beat carries me like a wind. I feel an amazing
sense of freedom and lightness. At times I feel
that my body is dancing by itself and yet I am in
full control, as one.*

Another woman dancer who is a practising psychic had this
experience:

*Dance exhilarating, ecstatic, danced with eyes
open – vast movements of energy – lifted –
jumping – wanted to fly.*

*Fell face down – total relaxation, couldn't move –
taken to mats to lie. Deep, deep, deep relaxation.
Felt held in the arms of the Bear of the West.*

*Then found myself in the mouth of an enormous
cave – hundreds of torch bearers – flaming
torches – like a Mayan temple – huge steps
leading upward. I was climbing them alone and
wondered if I was the sacrifice. Met huge figure
with vast Eagle's head. He asked me why I had
come and what I wished. I replied 'I wish to dance
in the realm of the Gods.' He took me to a stone
slab where I lay down. My head was chopped off
and out of my throat flew bats. These flew off
into the darkness of the void and I was one of
them. Then from a bat I turned into a crow. Then
I was human and crow. I was told that my power
and energy came from the womb – the void…
Then in a crow-like manner – still flying but in
human shape – I saw myself giving birth and out
of my vagina was spinning energy that seemed
like new stars and galaxies being born, but very
much the awareness that I was giving birth to
myself. Very powerful!!*

*Then I felt myself coming down to re-enter this
me. I was floating down to the left side of my
larger being. As I came back to this 'me' I felt I*

*brought with me a lot of wholeness and*
*completeness and power of the larger part of*
*the being that is me. It made all the mundane*
*problems of my life dissolve into insignificance.*

In a later dance she experienced this:

*...I felt the sound of the drum enter my feet and*
*move upward to my solar plexus. Once there*
*I actually became the sound, there was no*
*separation. I felt moments of bliss and knew that*
*I had become a kind of wave of sound. But while*
*the drums lasted it was as though I was caught*
*inside them and they wouldn't let me go. Then the*
*sound become very strong inside and was hurting*
*my stomach, like an animal biting at my sides,*
*but I couldn't get away from it. Then the*
*sensation and sound became so overwhelming*
*and so insistent I thought afterwards that had*
*someone not stopped me dancing I would have*
*just passed out.*

A week later she was able to interpret the dance:

*When I was in therapy four years ago and*
*working with my dreams, I had a recurring*
*dream of a man (an ex-boss) and the dreams were*
*very vivid but somehow I couldn't realize what*
*they were trying to tell me, even though we*
*discussed then at length how I felt about this*
*person in waking consciousness and what he*
*might symbolize in the dreams. He was always*

*a figure clothed in intrigue and fear. In 'real life'*
*he was a man with a very powerful temper.*
*Following the trance-dance I dreamed very vividly*
*of this person. But this time he greeted me and*
*embraced me and was my friend and helper.*
*When I woke I felt very different, a kind of inner*
*peace and calm... and a different quality of being.*
*When I asked myself what it was I came up with*
*the word 'fierce'. I felt very fierce and 'wolfish'.*

*Well, during the week I found myself in three*
*situations quite unplanned and not manouvered*
*by me where I found myself telling three people*
*what I thought of them and where they could go!*
*Out of my life!*

*Having suffered greatly through depression,*
*which is indeed self-directed anger in my case, I*
*have not until this time accepted my own anger*
*or known how to express it in a creative way.*

Another woman dancer had this experience of the Upper World
right at the end of a session:

*...the drummer started up a rapid rhythm. It*
*caught me like the wind catches a sail. I flapped*
*my arms to keep balance, but already was higher*
*off the ground than a second before. I kept*
*flapping my hands – I couldn't help it. An energy*
*ran through my body and moved it so quickly and*
*lightly. I was so excited I didn't know whether I*
*was laughing or crying, but my throat closed and*

139

*opened all at once. I made excited little sounds,*
*altogether too small for the rush of energy I was*
*feeling, and altogether too inhibited for the odd*
*display of now wildly flapping arms and hands.*
*My throat became sore as if wanting to scream,*
*but my training and conditioning would not allow*
*me... I was situated in front of the tray of candles*
*which was in the middle of the room. Never*
*moving my eyes from the flames, the candles all*
*receded far away, as though I had really jumped*
*out of the bounds of gravity, far up and away.*
*Indeed, the elevation now in my jump was such*
*that I felt like I was a trampoline – arms still*
*waving madly, throat aching to shout, body as*
*light as a feather, vision now quite blurred, and an*
*excitement rushing through my body which surely*
*a child feels when she is so thrilled she cannot*
*contain herself...It seemed the deeper I breathed,*
*the higher I could jump...Lifting myself so high*
*was as easy as breathing deeply, and then*
*suddenly it all went. I remember THINKING. That*
*was the fatal action and I came back to earth*
*with a bump. In an instant I knew I'd thought it*
*impossible to do what I was doing, and so it was!*

Compare these stories with those in the last chapter. It is interesting to see how human process unfolds similarly with different methods.

The induction I have described as best I can. It is something to be experienced. At first it can look quite alarming. However it is good to know that many seasoned dancers can induct themselves. The induction works both as a way to help the dancer spin out of mind-control and into the dance, into contact with the beat of the drum, and also it can help as a placebo to give a shy person an 'excuse' to act out of their normal self-limitations with the feeling 'I was pushed'!

Responses to the dance, as you can see in the above reports, are very different. Its beauty is that it allows the Spirit to take the dancer where the dancer needs to go, and it allows Spirit to know best without the interference of human know-alls. The facilitator's job is to respond to the needs of the dancer and to make the space as safe as possible both emotionally and physically.

# Relaxation

A place for relaxation is required with enough cushions, blankets and the like to make it comfortable for up to perhaps a quarter to a third of the participants at any one time. The relaxation follows when the dancer has quite simply had enough. Some dancers will lie down when exhausted, some collapse in a heap, and some gently walk off to the relaxation area. When they lay down where they are, four people are needed to gently take an arm and a leg each and carry them off to the relaxation area. In all cases it is good to have someone stay with them as long as they want, as feelings can come up to the surface and the person may need emotional support, or just something as simple as a glass of water. It is important to have enough facilitators to look after those for whom deep emotion is touched. Once the person is rested, they rejoin the circles of dancers and minders again.

# Integration

At the end of the whole session, we might have a period of light dancing, perhaps to something like reggae music – something quite different to the drums, and then sit down and share stories to integrate the experience and see what we learned, and get a sense of how the spirit moved us that day. Sharing stories is a very important part of integration because it helps provide a context for what may otherwise seem quite bizarre experiences.

I would like to stress that compared to those cultures which have not lost the ability to connect directly with the Spirit World, we are at a beginner's level with this work. In his wonderful book *Sangoma* (Touchstone, 1995), James Hall recounts his experience of going through a full African training to become a shaman and gain 'lidlotis', spirits who help him divine and know and thus heal. (This book is highly recommended!) Relative to such experience, we are beginners. It is good to remember that and stay humble whatever great visions we might experience. Many old cultures on this planet danced nightly. Some such as the Minianka in Mali still do. The shaman drummer 'drums' the dancers into a state of balance and harmony. (For more information on this read *The Healing Drum* by *Yaya Diallo*). Many of us spend our evenings watching television and we might think nightly trance-dancing an odd thing to do. What, I wonder, will our long-term descendants make of many of us spending night after night supinely watching television?

# SEVEN

# GIFTS FROM
# the Plant
# Kingdom

Let us be clear about one thing. Teacher plants are NOT necessary to the shamanic journey, or any other spiritual journey of awakening. However, they have been used by shamans for millennia as a teaching tool to help speed up the journey of the apprentice. If anything, I would call them catalysts. Look at it this way: plants give us oxygen, nutrition, shelter and medicine. We can all agree on that. Without the plant kingdom, we and all the animal kingdoms would not exist. Plants came before us and created the ecological system of the Earth. From that standpoint it is perhaps less of a shock to consider that they also give us consciousness-raising medicine. This knowledge has been suppressed for maybe 3000 years in Europe.

Teacher plants are great helpers to those who have difficulty opening to the cosmos. There are many ways of opening up, and for myself I need all the help I can get! Hence I have taken advantage of opportunities with plant medicines when possible. However I never take 'drugs' or mess with any mind-bombs. And I only take teacher plants when I am in the presence of and guided by someone who is a master of that plant. In that way I maintain a sensible level of safety.

There are many teacher plants which have been used to help open the senses and break the fixation of the external, seemingly-real world. Peyote is mainly used by North and some Central Americans; San Pedro cactus by the coastal and mountain Inca of Peru; Ayahuasca is the jungle medicine of the upper Amazon; Fly Agaric, the red and white mushroom, is used in the Lapland and other arctic places and is connected with the Father Christmas myth; Psylocybin is freely available in Britain; and around the world there are many, many other plants which bring the same gifts when correctly used.

It is interesting to look at the sacramental aspects of eating teacher plants. To quote Numi again, 'Ayahuasca is a way to take communion, like Christ's wine. It is an offering from the plant level.' (From *The World is as You Dream It*, by John Perkins).

# Wilderness Journey – My First Experience

My first experience with teacher plants happened in August 1980 on the journey in the Sierras I mentioned in the Introduction. I travelled from my then home in San Francisco to Bishop in East California to meet up with a group of people to go on my first ever wilderness journey. My inner being must have had some knowledge about the trip that I didn't, for I had slept increasingly fitfully as the time got closer and my inner dialogue really started examining my own madness for signing up for such a venture. Did I really want to do it? Was it worth all the trouble? It had taken a lot of effort to get all the bits and pieces needed together and I had borrowed a backpack and sleeping bag from a kind friend.

I met the group at a carpark 9000 feet high, a few miles outside the small town of Bishop. There they were – a motley looking crew of ordinary hikers, or so it looked, 12 in all. The leaders, Robert Greenway and Steve Harper, both were warm and welcoming people. The first thing we had to do was to pare down to the absolute minimum everything we were going to take. It was a three-day hike into the valley where we would camp and we had to take all our food with us. That meant there was room for little else. Well, I am something of a magpie and I tend to pack for all eventualities. But this time there was very little room left after my share of the food had been packed, and I was faced with having to carry this thing all the way on my back; I really learned about necessities. We were to dress for the climate simply by adding or subtracting layers of clothing, anything spare was just surplus weight. Finally the job was done. Three quarters of what I had brought was back in the car. 'We'll sleep here tonight,' announced Robert, 'It's too late to move.' Here? I thought. In a carpark? On hard ground?? There's a motel nine miles down the road with a soft bed! It was all I could do to hold my tongue and not say 'See you tomorrow!'

Over dinner, Robert said, 'Of course, a three day vision quest will be part of the journey.' A vision quest? 'And we will have a peyote ritual on our last night. And we will build a sweat lodge when we get there.' This easy, gentle trip suddenly turned into something very different. Peyote? All I knew about peyote was what I had read in Carlos Casteneda's books about how, under the influence of the plant, he had gyrated with a dog to the amusement of all present, and how he had later met Mescalito, the spirit of peyote. Well, if that was what was to happen, I would do my best to meet Mescalito too.

The first day we hiked about 2000 feet upwards, which is a long way at that altitude with a pack weighing more than 40 pounds. At least it was for me, 44 years old and a novice hiker. Because we camped above the tree line we were forbidden to have a fire – which meant there was no tea! Now this was a serious deprivation for a Brit! Yet I had chosen to come and I was paying for the 'pleasure'! I had not slept the first night in the carpark and I didn't sleep the next night either. I watched the whole progression of the stars and the Milky Way across the sky that night. The next day we took a beautiful walk up to the summit of Bishop Pass at 11,000 feet, along the high ground with its stunning views and down some way into the beginning of a valley. That evening we had a hot dinner with tea, and softer ground – relatively – to sleep on. Things were getting a little better, but I still didn't sleep a wink. The next afternoon we arrived at our destination, which was in a lovely valley with a stream at the bottom and some gorgeous mountains opposite.

The vision quest was a revelation to me. Instead of being bored to tears and perhaps scared half to death, I found myself making a new – or remaking an old but lost – connection with Mother Earth. During the night, the valley and the mountains came alive for me and I had a lovely conversation with some deer whose path I must have camped on. On the second night I ate about half a peyote button. It tasted fairly awful but I managed to get it down. Later in the night the mountain on the opposite side of the valley seemed to change. Its outline was the same but suddenly I was looking at lines of force. The best way I can describe it is to say that it appeared to me like the windings inside an electrical transformer – this was an ex-engineer's vision! Great lines of force that held the mountain's structure were visible to me. I looked around to check all the other directions, but they were just as normal. The vision was just in the mountain. Eventually I must have fallen asleep and in the morning the mountain was just a mountain!

A couple of nights later the group met for the peyote ceremony, high up above our camp at about 10,000 feet altitude. A big fire had been prepared in the shape of an arrow pointing east, the direction in which we would be 'travelling'. Some of the peyote had been made into tea, the rest was in the form of dried buttons. The ceremony began, the powers were called and we began our chants. Each person in turn led the circle, singing chants and shaking the rattle while the person to their right played the water drum. This drum is a cast iron pot with a skin stretched over it which is kept wet. The resulting sound seemed to me quite puny until I realized that it was just as loud inside my head as outside, and also that it made little or no difference how far away I was from it. The total effect of the peyote, the water drum and rattle, the fire and the chanting, combined with the fact that it was a night ceremony lasting from dusk till dawn, made it profoundly affecting.

However I must admit that on this night I did not approach the event in quite the most balanced way. I thought that if I was clever enough to 'see' the inside of the mountain with the aid of only half a peyote button, perhaps I really could meet Mescalito, or even see into the Universe, if only I could get enough peyote inside me! Needless to say I did not voice this thought to anyone. I had already been told it was very important to speak reverently when in earshot of the peyote otherwise its spirit might take a dislike to us. At the time this was not an idea to which my overly rational mind gave much credence.

The peyote tea was served as soon as the ceremony got going and I drank plenty of it. It tasted awful, but I got it down. Then came the dried buttons. These tasted even worse. They were chewy like old leather and the more I ate the worse they tasted. The experience I had was that at the beginning they tasted awful, then dreadful, then each additional piece tasted frightful, sickening, abominable, abysmal, excruciating, excoriating… and after that it got really bad!

Actually I didn't get very far that night. By about the third round of chants I felt myself really going somewhere inside myself, to a new place of consciousness perhaps. But then suddenly I had the feeling of a giant door inside my head, like the thick, heavy door of a bank strongroom, slamming shut with a resounding crunch. I was suddenly thrust back into everyday reality feeling terrible. My stomach felt as if it was the end of the world. It was so cold that I couldn't leave the fire and from that time on I had a truly dreadful night, unable to be properly sick. Dawn seemed never to come! In the morning I ate a little of the celebration fruit breakfast, then vomited my heart and guts out. After that I felt wonderful. This experience was a very forcible lesson to me to treat teacher plants with the utmost respect and not to think I could use them to be clever or to gain power for my own benefit.

# Shamanic Counselling Experiences – Drug Problems

A friend sent her 17-year-old son to me for counselling. He had been taking drugs and to finance his habit had been dealing to his fellow school pupils. He had been caught and things were serious. I listened to him and chatted about some of my experiences and did all I could to help him feel I was open and not a 'standard adult'. I asked him what he got out of the drugs and he described a blissful experience of 'oneness' the first time he took the drug – I think it was ecstasy. What he described was a classic, beautiful, 'Kensho'; a first awakening, an experience of awakening to the feeling of being in a living cosmos and being a loved part of it, and being held in the arms of All-That-Is. So, naturally, he took the drug another time to try and repeat the experience, only this time it wasn't quite as good. Again he tried, again it wasn't as good. So he upped the dose and tried again but still it wasn't the same. He upped the dose again and this time nasty, frightening images came to him. He took it yet again and this time the experience was really scary.

Compare this experience to a first visit to a psychotherapist. Suppose you are lonely and rather lost and feel no one understands you or even really listens to you. Suppose your parents had stopped listening to you around puberty – not such an unusual situation. Then you go to a psychotherapist and they listen and really want to hear what you feel and think. For what seems like the first time in your young life, someone actually wants to listen to you instead of just criticizing you! This can be a blissful experience too. To actually be heard and validated instead of torn to pieces. Wow! Next week you go again and it's good, but not quite the same blissful experience. The following week it seems to somehow get a little more difficult… and then each week it gets progressively harder. Where has the gloss gone? Really difficult issues start to surface, all that repressed fear and grief and rage. Just like a dark trip! Only with a therapist you have a live human consciousness there to help and guide you. Someone who has been through the mill and knows the mindscape. With a substance, powerful as it is, you have no reflection except your own, so when the repressed, dark emotions come up they seem like monsters from the deep, out of control, and you feel alone in confronting them.

*Teacher plants are a gift from the plant kingdom to be used in a sacred way for gaining knowledge of the universe. Drugs are potentially lethal substances and likely to bring destruction when taken without care and awareness.*

There is a great difference between natural plant medicines and synthesized laboratory drugs. My friend Howard Charing (*see Chapter 5*) related to me how he took a shamanic journey to meet the Spirit Of Ayahuasca – and found he did indeed meet a conscious Plant-Spirit who showed him an alternative reality. When he tried the same with LSD he found no spirit at all, just deadness and fantasy. Another difference is that only a major masochist could possibly get addicted to the plant medicines as they all taste awful and their effects on the stomach are usually far from pleasant.

There is a madness in using mind-food as recreation. It isn't intended for fun and spacing out, it is serious stuff. I know many people who have said that early drug experiences put them on a new road of life and broke up their rigid beliefs about what was what, but none that I can think of who looked back on the experience without a shudder of some kind. These are mind-bombs. Would you practise juggling with hand grenades? Play polo with a nuclear bomb? Almost everything has its rightful place and when used as nature intended will bring beneficial results. For example, heroin is a killer and morphine is metaphorically a life-saver in that it saves lives from unbearable pain – but they are basically the same substance. To use teacher plants in a sacred way in sacred ceremony can be a most beneficial and consciousness-expanding experience, bringing blissful experiences of oneness, of how we are all connected to everything, of the love that is at the basis of all existence.

One day I got a strange telephone call from a man who sounded deeply troubled. He had taken too many mushrooms, he said, and needed some specialist help. My name is 'out there', so to speak, so I get a few calls from people looking for assistance. Sometimes they expect me to have Castaneda-like powers. This man's story was that he had taken 250 mushrooms, the little English liberty caps. He had lost his sense of being grounded and was seeing things crawling around in his food, making it very difficult for him to eat. He had signed himself into a mental hospital for two days to rest up and recover, and then signed out again. He thought I could help. I got him talking and what came out was a heavy duty agenda for self-destruction. He was in a state of severe self-hatred. It saddens me

*151*

that I find so many people who expect to be healed from this kind of state without having to do any work themselves. The idea that a shaman or magician can fix illness without any effort on the patient's part is simply irresponsible. The work I did was to help the man see his own state, to take responsibility for himself and use his will to change his ways – which included laying off the mushrooms or anything else. I also worked on his energy field and his assemblage point to help him into a better balance with himself, from which he could take himself on and confront his self-pity. A couple of months later he came back to me again, this time with an uncle who was looking after him, and he was getting to grips with his life.

# *Vine of the Soul*

Ayahuasca is the jungle medicine of the upper Amazon. It is made from the ayahuasca vine (*Banisteriopsis Caapi*) and the leaf of the Chacruna plant (*Psychotria Viridis*). The two together make a potent visionary medicine. The vine contains harmala and harmaline which are short term MAO (monoamine oxidase) inhibitors, and the leaf contains DMT (N, N-dimethyl-tryptamine) – vision-inducing alkaloids. As with all natural medicines, the plant is a mixture of many alkaloids and that makes its properties unique. Chemistry doesn't explain everything. Peyote, for example, is said to contain 32 active alkaloids, so when just one of those alkaloids, mescaline (LSD) is synthesized in a laboratory, the result is not the same, contrary to popular opinion.

Ayahuasca is a name derived from two Quechua words: *aya* meaning spirit, ancestor, dead person, and *huasca* meaning vine or rope; hence it is known as *vine of the dead* or *vine of the soul*. It is also known by many other local names including *yaje, caapi, natema, pinde, pilde, daime, mihi,* and *dapa.* It plays a central role in the spiritual, religious and cultural traditions of the Indigenous and Mestizo (or mixed blood) peoples of the Upper Amazon, the Orinoco plains and the Pacific coast of Colombia and Equador. During the past few decades its shamanic and religious use has spread to urban areas of Colombia, Peru and Brazil. It is also known as *La Purga* because it is a formidable purge, as I personally experienced. Vomiting is to be expected!

The plants are collected from the rainforest in a sacred way and it is said that a shaman can find plentiful sources of the vine by listening for the 'drumbeat' that emanates from them. The mixture is prepared by cutting the vines to cookable lengths, scraping and cleaning them, then pounding them into a pulp. Meanwhile the Chacruna leaves are picked and cleaned. In the Santo Daime tradition of Brazil, the men prepare the vine and the women the leaves, chanting or singing hymns, as Santo Daime is a Christian path. The plants are then placed in a large pot, in a ratio of about two parts vine to one part leaves, and boiled until they make a golden brown, slightly viscous liquid which looks rather like badly made drinking chocolate!

There are variations in the particular brews favoured by different shamans and different traditions. Sometimes the leaves of the *Psychotria Cartaghinensis* or the *Diplopterys Cabrerana* are used instead of the *viridis*. This, I think, is depends upon what is available in different places. Sometimes tobacco is added and sometimes also datura. I have tasted quite 'sweet' brews such as Santo Daime – I say 'sweet' in quotes because none of it tastes nice, rotted drinking chocolate is not a bad analogy. I have also tasted really foul brews with tobacco juice and probably datura, a very poisonous hallucinogen, though I was unable to get precise confirmation at the time as to just what was in the potion. Sometimes the brews become fermented which makes them particulary foul, but the shamans think nothing of it and apparently the effects are just the same.

Sadly, due to the increasing popularity of ayahuasca, ready supplies of the plants are becoming more difficult to find. 'Progress' is taking its toll even in this. There is now a need to cultivate the vine and for it to be harvested only by those who know how to do so properly, without damage to the plant.

Most Amazonian shamanic traditions teach that the ayahuasca spirits will transmit their power and knowledge only to those willing to undergo a long and stringent initiation process involving a strict diet and sexual abstinence. When I was in Pucallpa, Peru, experiencing ayahuasca with local Shipibo shamans, I met a man from New York who was going through just such an initiation, living on a salt, sugar and lots-of-other-things-free diet. It is actually easier to say what is allowed than what is not. The diet basically consists of boiled plantain – a very dull vegetable – white fish and white rice; all with no flavourings whatever, though many devotees add other simple foods. I experienced this diet for a week in the jungle and I lost weight, energy and all interest in eating (and dreamed of baked beans on toast!). Sexual abstinence would be no problem on this diet! It is said that when an initiate follows these conditions and takes ayahuasca several times a week (three or four times seems to be the average), with the focussed intent of learning from the Spirits, only then will the Spirits give of their knowledge.

I experienced a healing session while in Pucallpa with Benito and Guillermo Arevalo. Their temple is the patio behind their very modest house which lies off a dirt road. As well as being visited by local people there were some from as far away as Lima. Almost everyone present drank the brew, and then rested for the hour or so before anything happened. The healing began with each person coming forward in turn to be diagnosed by the shamans who, with the aid of the ayahuasca, were able to 'see'. Medicines were prescribed and changes to lifestyle and diet recommended where needed. I noticed that compared to the apprentice training sessions I had attended, the visions played a less important part, which showed just how much the shaman, with chanting and music of one sort or another, actually induces and controls the visions.

Auahuasca is also used just as a medicine. Its purging ability is useful for the purging of illness and cleansing of parasites. The 'morning after' effect is one of purity and simplicity. One experiences a lovely feeling of awakeness and presence, nothing whatever like the 'morning after' effect of alcohol or drugs.

So what, perhaps, is the advantage of ayahuasca over other disciplines? In the words of Padrino Alex Polari de Alverga, leader of the Santo Daime Community in Brazil:

> *Daime (ayahuasca) is basically a shortcut. It's as*
> *if we had been travelling down the same highway*
> *as the rest of humanity, but then, in order to*
> *arrive at our destination more quickly we took a*
> *side road. When taking such a shortcut, however,*
> *we must be very careful and clearminded. It is a*
> *shortcut that leads us to truth, but only if we*
> *follow in the footsteps of the Masters who have*
> *preceded us.*

Medicines like ayahuasca can help us along our path but we still have to do the work ourselves. It feels to me as if ayahuasca is an extremely powerful ally who will take us places, although we need groundedness and stability to handle its power and to be able to use it wisely. Usually the first step is to the 'Lower World', where we go into a 'death' place of despair and hopelessness, into our shadow of old unworked-through trauma and pain. Ayahuasca induces us to vomit up and evacuate out both literally and metaphorically! When this step is completed, we are taken to the 'Upper World' where we experience beautiful visions of connection to creation and its many mansions of exquisite existence. (*Compare this with the experiences of trance-dancers in Chapter 6 and journeyers in Chapter 5*). Of course we go back and forth from Upper to Lower. Ayahuasca is a tricky, deceptive, deceitful ally. Just when you think you've got everything perfectly set up for a really lovely journey all sorts of surprises appear. It is a great teacher of how to 'expect the unexpected without expectation!'

## *Ayahuasca Journeys*

Ayahuasca stalked me! At least that's how it felt. Out of the blue one day in 1992 I received a phone call from a Brazilian anthropologist who was in London for a few weeks. He came to visit and we chatted for three hours about life, the universe and shamanism, and then he mentioned that he wanted to arrange an ayahuasca ceremony with some friends. I was just waiting for the right moment to get myself invited when he said he needed a quiet place to hold the ceremony. 'I have just the place,' I said, and showed him my front room which I have been using for therapy and ceremony since 1983. We held the ceremony a few days later. My friend had been involved with the Santo Daime group in Brazil and the ceremony was a wonderful mixture of Christian hymns sung mainly in Spanish, and native-style ceremony. The visions were lovely, like a tapestry of art flowing and constantly changing. It was like looking into the fabric of creation, but delicately, and intensely colourfully.

Very shortly after this experience two friends brought an apprentice of Agustin Rivas, the Peruvian mestizo shaman, to England and another ceremony took place in my front room. However I was eager to further my experience with the plant in its natural habitat, so I went with a group of friends to Peru in the summer of 1993 for a jungle experience.

# *Jungle Journey*

My journey to Peru in 1993 began with three weeks in Pucallpa with my friend and guide Peter Cloudsley, and ended with two weeks at Yushintaita, the jungle retreat of Agustin Rivas. In Pucallpa, Peter and I went searching for shamans and found them most easily. All teaching in this area is done through ayahuasca and open meetings begin at about nine in the evening, usually on Tuesdays or Fridays! I experienced several ceremonies with my friends Benito and Guillermo whom I mentioned above, but will recount in detail just one which was with a cousin of theirs called don Matteo, who lives in the nearby village of San Francisco on the shores of Lake Yarinacocha.

Peter and I went to the harbour in Yarina and caught a boat to San Francisco, a Shipibo village, about an hour and a quarter's ride along the lake shore. We stayed at a lakeside house, La Perla, with our host Tomas. We took blankets and anoraks as although the days are warm, the 'Frio de San Juan', a cold wind, was blowing and the

157

nights got surprisingly chilly. It was dusk when we arrived at San Francisco and we saw no village, just a mud trail from the lakeside. However the boat people assured us it was the right way. Full of doubt, we walked about a quarter of a mile further and suddenly at the crest of a slope there to our right lay the village. We asked directions to don Matteo's house and some obliging children led us there. However there seemed to be something strange about the house they pointed to as we crested a rise. There was an eerie glow coming from it. Did this mean Matteo was a master shaman and in such strong contact with the spirits that his house glowed? Was a UFO visiting the house? As we got closer we could dimly see in the flickering glow that people were sitting on the floor of the house all facing the same direction. Soon all was revealed. They were watching a small black and white battery-operated television! The Peru versus Uruguay match was in full swing and continued so for the next two hours. Our ceremony had to wait until the end of the match. That's progress! (The result was 2–1 to Uruguay!)

After the match the family went to bed. Shipibo (a local indigenous tribe) houses consist of a single room with a thatched roof, open on three sides to the weather. The floor is a simple wooden platform about two feet above the ground. The family simply climbed into their mosquito nets and went to sleep right beside us. Taking part in the ceremony there was just Matteo, his assistant, Peter, and myself. Matteo picked up a shabby looking plastic bottle and poured some of the disgusting looking contents into a cup and handed it to Peter. He offered the next cup to me and I took a deep breath, made a silent prayer and drank. Ugh! I shuddered; my body did not like the stuff. Matteo and his assistant drank next, completely calmly, and then we all settled down to rest and meditate for the hour or so before the spirit came.

I was brought out of my reverie by the sound of very gentle, beautiful, falsetto singing. It was Matteo. It was getting very cold and I wrapped myself up as best I could and leant against one of the poles which held up the roof. Matteo's extraordinarily beautiful singing brought me visions of exquisite geometric patterns in fabulous colours flowing across my mindscape, constantly moving and changing. At one point it felt as if the music was being converted into a visual kaleidoscopic experience in my mind and I 'saw' notes moving across my mind's eye. My stomach rumbled ominously from time to time but I had little feeling of nausea, although by morning I had been thoroughly purged. At one point I lay down to shield myself from the cold wind and I felt certain Matteo was singing right in front of my forehead. It was a beautiful experience, the visions were magnificent as I watched a kaleidoscope of what could have been South American weaving designs. I sat up to check his position and discovered he was huddled up facing the other way. As soon as I lay down again his singing once again was just in front of my third eye – or was it ? No, it felt more as if it was inside my head rather than outside.

I noticed lying down that my body went into a sort of minor paralysis. If I deliberately chose and willed myself to move, then I could, but when I lay still, parts of me felt paralysed. Later in the night I felt a very special feeling around my solar plexus. A feeling of incredible warmth and loving connection to the Universe and everything around, everything in existence, a feeling of the greatest wellbeing. Suddenly I remembered this feeling from long, long ago. As a little child I had experienced this. I was not alone, I was part of all this. It all loved me and I loved all existence.

Later I experienced pressure on my crown chakra and then on my third eye. It felt as if some healing was taking place. Then my ears

*159*

became 'closed', I became afraid and they 'popped' back to normal. I wondered if I had unintentionally stopped something happening and thought about just how much I still have to work with the enemy of fear.

# *Life is What Happens While You're Busy Making Other Plans*

## *(John Lennon)*

Early in the morning, at first light, we were offered a boat back to Yarina. There we changed to a crowded boat which would take us home to La Perla along the lake shore the other way. By then it was about seven in the morning. I was pretty shattered and looking forward to some warmth, tea and sleep when I noticed a pair of lovely dark eyes looking at me, and below them a beautiful warm, amused smile. She said something to me in Spanish and I must have looked bewildered because my Spanish is just fit for a restaurant menu. A man sitting next to me translated. 'She said she wants to make a baby with you.' I must have looked even more bewildered – I don't get offers like that everyday. 'She wants to know how old you are,' said the man. I looked at her properly, a quite beautiful young woman of part-Quechua, part-Spanish descent, I guessed. Half my age at the most. '27,' I said and laughed. 'That's my age,' she said. This conversation continued in full view of and to the great amusement of the other boat passengers as every line was translated. We exchanged names. She was called Birta. I reached out my hand to her and we held hands like teenagers and looked in each other's eyes for the rest of the trip, while communicating through this kindly public translation line. Soon the journey ended and Peter and I got off at La Perla. She was going further to the next village. I didn't ask to see her again and we left Pucallpa a few days after. Later I found out she was the local school teacher and was on her way to the village school.

At the end of my journey in Peru I can remember trying to piece together the many lessons I had received. I had travelled there with the intention of opening myself to the Spirit World, of attempting to move through what felt like blocks to my ability to deeply connect with the subtle realms... perhaps to forget conveniently any blocks I might have to connecting to the everyday, to people... to the feminine! I realized that while I had been busy looking for increased awareness and connection in one direction, the Universe had shown me my unawareness by serving up an unexpected invitation from another, which I had missed. I remember reflecting sadly on many other such possibilities which I had missed in my life through being 'busy with other plans'.

EIGHT

# SHAMANISM
# Today

When viewing the whole field of self-development from the shamanistic point of view, everyone is on a self-development path. That is inherent in being alive! We are each minuscule particles of All-That-Is, the Great Spirit, and part of the Great Spirit is on a path of development though three-dimensional life experience. Or to put it another way: Planet Earth is God's growth group!

We could say that All-That-Is is busy experiencing itself through all life forms, one of which is us. Therefore to consciously enter the shamanic path you simply need to be a human being seeking to know Self and to understand the Universe. It is about walking life's path with the intention of developing awareness and consciousness, about making the choice to be self-responsible with the aim of acquiring knowledge, with the desire to learn 'the Way of the Lord' which means Divine Law; or in other words how the universe (God) really works.

As a shamanic healer and therapist, I find that almost everyone I am called on to help is suffering in some way from lack of self-esteem and difficulty in 'dreaming' a healthy, contented and harmonious life into manifestation. Their personal mythology is usually one which includes feelings of self-doubt, of being unlovable, of worthlessness and sometimes pointlessness. These kind of feelings are the spiritual-emotional crisis of the Western world. We encounter plenty of false ego and self-inflation, but how often do we meet someone who is truly at one with themselves, at ease with their emotional self and their sexuality, grounded in their physical body, at one with their life journey?

Healing is not just for oneself, however, we are all parts of a culture. The culture itself is sick and the only way to heal the culture is to heal the separate members of that culture, and that means you and me. The Native American saying *omitaquaye oyasin* means 'For all my relations'. It is traditional to say this in prayer when entering a sweatlodge to purify oneself, and at other sacred moments. We are saying 'I go through this healing not just for myself but for all I am related to.' And who is that? It is my blood relatives, it is all my human brothers and sisters, it is my animal kin, plant kin, rock kin, it is the whole planet herself. I am related to all that exists. While I am out of balance, depressed, sad, angry, violent, I am a force for imbalance, for anti-life, ('evil') and in need of healing. As I heal and balance myself, I become a force for good ('God') and for the healing of others. My healing contributes to the healing of the whole.

In the West self-discovery is often confused with self-indulgence. The work involved in revealing the truth of oneself, healing the old wounds and traumas and coming to a place of balance and harmony within, demands courage and fortitude. It is the very reverse of indulgence.

The old ideology is that one should be out there *doing* in the world – changing, moving, having an effect, 'proving' oneself, becoming famous, 'achieving' – without necessarily needing any self-discovery, self-reflection or development of inner life. In other words one should maintain ignorance of self and go out and create change for others! We see the result of such behaviour and attitudes all around us in pollution, destruction, unnecessary consumption, increasingly empty media and entertainment, profiteering, and the steady and unrelenting decimation of the planetary infrastructure as if by a vast gang of ignorant morons.

Take a look at yourself for a moment. What brought you to a path of self-healing? Did you reach a point of despair? Did life take you deep into yourself and force you to ask difficult questions about your existence, your worth, your relationships to other people, to the planet, the point of it all? Rarely does anyone step onto a path to seek the Light without an experience in the Dark. For myself it was the periods of deep despair and loneliness that propelled me to find something worthwhile in life.

Here are some classic ways to work with the stuff of oneself:

## Habits

There is a wonderful piece in Casteneda's *Journey to Ixtlan* (Simon & Schuster), where don Juan mercilessly teases Casteneda about his routines, especially his habit of eating regularly whether he is hungry or not. Disrupting our routines helps us to stay awake. Get out of the other side of bed, go to work a different route, eat when you are hungry, not because it's (lunch)time, get into some different social activities, listen for the spaces between sounds, look at the shadows rather than the foreground, challenge your addictions and habitual behaviours, eat less and enjoy becoming lighter. Cut out refined sugars from your diet. When we do these kind of things emotional garbage comes to the surface and tries to get us back to old ways. Call on the Spirit to help stay steadfast. Waking up is not easy or comfortable.

## Daily practices

Listen to nudges, hunches, omens, odd happenings, seeming coincidences, synchronicity. Having no fixed habits and routines means that one can be more available for the 'nudges of spirit', those little moments of knowing, of information that just comes. Silent times, meditative times, help us to become available to spirit. Too much busy-ness is an enemy to this (and one I have 'given away', sought to change, in my Full Moon Fire Ceremony so many times!). Prayer is about communicating from oneself to spirit; meditation is about giving spirit a chance to communicate to you. It is good to take time for both – but only when the spirit moves you, rather than as a habit. Unless, of course, you are a disorganized person whose routines are irregular and who has difficulty sticking to anything. In that case for you a change of habit would be to have regular disciplines!

## Shamanic journeying

Once you have learned to journey, perhaps at a workshop, it is good practice to take journeys frequently to develop your access to and communication with the Lower and Upper worlds. A simple pocket cassette player with earphones and a shamanic drumming tape is helpful. Howard Charing and I have made a tape for this (*see Resources*).

## Gazing

All the television and radio stations are playing right where you are, but you neither hear nor see them unless you turn on and tune in the television or radio. All organic, living beings have electromagnetic auras, energy fields, but you don't see them unless you change your state of consciousness (that is, tune your instrument!). We only see a small range of light frequency and hear a small range of sound frequency. We don't even see ultra violet or infra red. Scientific materialists like to say that if you can't see it, hear it or feel it, it isn't there. Well, *gazing* is a good exercise to practise extending perception past that limitation. Look into the shadows; listen to the emptiness between sounds; let your eyes be unfocused; when you see people, gaze just past them. This exercise is a great challenge for scientists, materialists, workaholics and control freaks!

## Do something for someone else

Give service. 'Practise Random Kindness And Senseless Acts Of Beauty!'

Whilst these are ways to work on one's own, *the shamanic path is walked with a teacher and a group.* It cannot be done by mail order! We need teachers – people who have walked the path before us – and we need companions on the journey who will be our mirrors, giving us the reflections we need, though maybe not always the ones we want!

# Questions

In this section I will try and answer some typical questions I get asked:

*Is shamanism a New Age religion?*

No it is not a religion at all. It involves no beliefs, it is a spiritual path to knowledge. New Age? – Hardly, it is 40 – 50,000 years old! It is far more correct to say that the Alternative Scene and so-called New Age is a shamanistic revival!

*All this New Age spirituality seems to be a load of DIY ideas. How can you believe in all this?*

Of course it's DIY! All proper spirituality is DIY! If you do not do it yourself, someone else does it for you and that means you are not taking responsibility for yourself! Spirituality is a search for knowledge through experience, an ongoing exploration into the world of

Spirit, into the way the Universe works, into the 'Mind Of God'. You are the only person who can do that for you. And it is not about believing anything, it is about gaining knowledge and learning from experience.

*What are your spiritual/religious beliefs?*

As explained through this book, I do my best to access knowledge, not beliefs. However, this question usually has a subtext which reads along the lines of 'Do you think the same as I do so we can support each other's comfortable prejudices, or differently in which case I must prove you wrong!' The question suggests that the questioner may be stuck in a dogmatic belief system rather than open-mindedly seeking truth.

*Why do you work with Native American and other foreign paths?*
*What right have you to these teachings when it's not your culture?*

Firstly I am a citizen of Planet Earth! That is my culture. Secondly – go back in history far enough and all my ancestors, like yours, lived in shamanic cultures. And just because a people live in a certain place on the earth doesn't mean they have always lived there. Who are the British? A mixture of Angles, Saxons, Romans, Vikings, Gauls and Celts – and that's just for starters. The native north American people came partially from the Mongols and also from the Maya, Aztec and other tribes of Central and south America. Some Celts emigrated from Europe to the Americas a very long time ago so there is a connection between the old ways of this land and theirs. And once we go back though the mists of time to Atlantis we find a lot more unlikely connections between seemingly disparate peoples. The Jews (pale skinned) could well have come from Scotland or Lapland and moved down to the Middle East at the time of the flood!

I have another answer to this question, namely that this path happened to come my way through Native American teachers when I lived in San Francisco, and it touched me greatly. And who am I to refuse a gift of spirit? Also, the old ways of Britain have been so decimated over the centuries by power-hungry religion that an enormous amount of our culture has been lost. The Native American people have managed to maintain much of their knowledge and many of their medicine people have received visions indicating that this is the time they are to teach people of any colour or race who come with an open heart. Medicine people are concerned with the colour of the person's heart, not their skin.

Also, as described earlier in this book, the old ways share a common world view. It is the details that are culturally different.

Here is something to remember. The word holocaust is usually used to mean the terrible tragedy that occurred in Germany in the last war. It is also good to remember that to the Native American people 'holocaust' describes the systematic decimation of their culture, the loss of their lands and their right to live in their own way, the loss of their rights to their own traditions and even language that have taken place over the last five hundred years. Shamefully, in many places this is still going on. It is a tribute to their incredible generosity of spirit that they are making their ancient wisdom available to help many people heal themselves, including descendants of their conquerors.

*People are coming up with all sorts of prophecies: 'Planet Earth is changing vibration / we are about to enter a Pleiadian photon belt where everything will be changed / Maitreya the Christ is coming and we should all follow him / Jesus is returning / UFOs will soon be bringing space people to take over / the Mayan calendar ends in 2012*    **169** *and that's that... Why not just wait for it to happen instead of doing all this work on yourself?*

Since when has anything worked on Planet Earth by abdication of responsibility? If the Planet is to change vibration, how is that going to happen if we humans, who are part of Earth after all, don't change our vibration? Last time Jesus came it didn't exactly make life easier for anyone, why should it if he or some such teacher comes again? We have had years of dogmatic religion telling people to believe and it hasn't solved human problems. Planet Earth is a school of experience and she teaches responsibility, she teaches giving and receiving, she teaches that our deepest beliefs and thoughts manifest in time and that we are responsible for the experiences we create. There is no way not to do the work for yourself. Abdication of responsibility is a negative choice which brings its own karma.

I feel that there is a deep-level change going on and that the spirit world is giving us vast help to raise our consciousness and do something about the mess we have created on the planet. But I also feel that some of the current millennial ideas of a sudden change to a new vibration and a great ascension to a Garden of Eden-like life are based, in part at least, on an understandable human desire to avoid having to face the very real enormity of our situation.

*What might I learn in a Shamanic Workshop?*

You can learn the ancient techniques of journeying to other worlds, of changing your state of consciousness in order to travel, of meeting spirit guides and power animals and touching wisdom deep within. You can learn to retrieve soul parts for another and in the process you learn how much we are connected on the other plains of consciousness.

You can enter the wonderful realm of the dance and learn to get out of your head and into your body and the rhythm of life. You can experience different states of awareness and find vibrancy and 'being-ness' in your body that you may not have been aware of for a long time.

You can heal and re-balance the inner child and heal old wounds. This is the south and the first prerequisite for going further with your journey. Whether you do this under the title of psychotherapy or shamanism, or whatever method you choose, until the inner healing happens and leads you to a place of taking yourself on and no longer blaming others – your parents, the world, the system or god – you are not ready to go too much further.

You can enter the magical Sweatlodge, the womb of Mother Earth, and reconnect with ancestral and ancient feelings and memories and with the elemental kingdoms.

You can Vision Quest on the mountain or in the valley, knowing you are supported by people at base camp and that you are guided through the stages of the quest, to your own learning from it, whatever that might be.

You can learn to extend your perception, feel auras, and interact with other people's energy fields. You can learn that you do not end at your skin, that your physical body is just the visible part of you, that your energy field touches the world.

You can participate in a year-long course like 'Elements Of Shamanism' (*see Resources*), which is a guided journey around the medicine wheel, touching all points and showing you many aspects of yourself, your life journey and your connection with Mother Earth, Father Sky and All-That-Is.

In effect, you can choose and direct a personal re-education programme to take you back to yourself, back into connection with
your instinctual nature and with your spiritual self, back into connection with the Earth and the Cosmos. And I cannot think of
anything more worthwhile to do with one's life at this present time
of great world crisis and opportunity.

The end is always also a beginning. Let me conclude with my
heyeokah creation story:

> *Once upon a no-time, in a no-place, nowhere*
> *Lived Absolutely-Nothing.*
> *In this nowhere place, nothing always happened*
> *As it had done for all eternity,*
> *And Absolutely Nothing was absolutely fed-up!*
>
> *So, on one auspicious no-day when the stars,*
> *Had there been any stars,*
> *Would have been in perfect alignment,*
> *Absolutely-Nothing decided to split itself into two*
> *So it could meet itself and see its own reflection.*
>
> *And so it split itself into two parts,*
> *Two equal and opposite Somethings, as after all,*
> *One can only create something out of nothing in*
>     *this way.*
> *And one was called yin, or feminine,*
> *And the other yang, or masculine.*

*And the two now looked at each other*
*And were deeply attracted for they were*
    *complementary,*
*And they were also deeply repelled for they*
    *were different,*
*And so they began a dance,*

*And they danced towards each other,*
*And they danced away from each other,*
*And as they danced they swayed and spun around*
    *and around,*
*They laughed and they laughed with the pure joy*
    *of being.*

*Absolutely-Nothing was so pleased that now*
*Something was happening,*
*And it realized it was now not nothing any longer*
*But Absolutely Everything.*
*This realization brought so much joy that*
    *laughter came from deep within.*
*And as the great feminine and the great*
    *masculine*
*Spun and spun,*
*Such great laughter came forth that could*
    *not be contained,*
*Such joy that it had to burst forth.*

*And it did, in a GREAT BIG BANG.*
*And so Everything became a Universe in space*
    *and time.*

And cutting a very, very long story very, very, very short, somewhere about twelve to fifteen or more billion Earth-years later, here we are, not bored at all, dreaming a great dream, enjoying a great play, walking a Great Journey…

# RESOURCES

# *Books*

## *Anthologies and teachings*

Gary Doore (ed.). *The Shaman's Path*, Shambala, 1988
Nineteen chapters by practitioners and researchers in the wide field of shamanism: Stanley Krippner, Michael Harner, Jeanne Achterberg, Stanislav Grof and Joan Halifax among others.

Shirley Nicholson (ed.). *Shamanism*, Quest, 1987
Another compilation with 20 chapters, some by the same people but also including Serge King on Hawaiian Huna, Ralph Metzner, Brooke Medicine Eagle, John Redtail Freesoul and Jean Houston.

Kenneth Meadows. *The Medicine Way*, Element Books, 1990
An excellent book which lays out the ground of shamanistic teachings of the Native Americans. It covers the alchemy of the Four Directions, and gives a number of exercises and tasks to help the seeker on his or her journey. Also: *Shamanic Experience, Earth Medicine, Where Eagles Fly*, and *Rune Power*.

Joan Halifax, PhD. *Shaman, The Wounded Healer*, Thames & Hudson, 1982
A beautifully illustrated book, full of rich quotations and pictures of shamans and their art. Many ancient wise ones are quoted. Also: *Shamanic Voices*.

Michael Harner. *The Way of the Shaman*, Bantam Press, 1980
The author's experiences with the Jivaro and the Conibo in the Amazon jungle, and his distillation of a shaman's work and the states of consciousness experienced.

Victor Sanchez. *The Teachings of Don Carlos*, Bear & Co., 1995
Masterful extrapolation of the works of Carlos Casteneda. Also: *Toltecs of the New Millenium*, Bear & Co., 1996

Felicitas D. Goodman. *Where Spirits Ride the Wind – Trance Journeys and Other Ecstatic Experiences*, Indiana University Press, 1990
A fascinating account of the author's work with sacred postures and the spirits we can connect with.

Roger N. Walsh. *The Spirit of Shamanism,* Mandala, 1990

Steven Foster and Meredith Little. *The Book of the Vision Quest*, Bear Tribe Publications, 1980
A bible for all vision questers.

Ed McGaa Eagleman. *Mother Earth Spirituality*, HarperCollins, 1990

Mercia Eliade. *Shamanism: Archaic Techniques of Ecstasy*, Penguin, 1989

Leo Rutherford, *Your Shamanic Book*, Piatkus, 2001.

Sandra Ingermann. *Soul Retrieval*, Harper San Francisco, 1991

Thomas E. Mails. *Fools Crow – Wisdom and Power*, Council Oak Books, 1991
The wisdom of a highly respected shaman elder of the Teton Sioux. Also:
*Mystic Warriors of the Plains*.

Arnold Mindell. *The Shaman's Body,* Harper San Francisco, 1993

Sedonia Cahill and Joshua Halpern. *The Ceremonial Circle*, Mandala, 1991

## *Personal experiences and autobiographies*

Carlos Castaneda. *Journey to Ixtlan* and seven other titles, Penguin Books
This is my favourite of Casteneda's works; it covers the early period in his
apprenticeship and includes the basis of the teachings he received. There is
much controversy about the authenticity of his work and I recommend any
sceptics read the following:

Tom Brown Jnr. *The Vision*, *The Quest* and *The Journey*, Berkley Books, 1988
The wonderful story of the author's apprenticeship as a young white boy to
an Apache shaman of great wisdom. It is easy to feel one is there going
through the experiences with him. As he writes with hindsight, Tom Brown is
able to explain his experiences and they are more comprehensible than
Casteneda, though no less extraordinary.

Alberto Villoldo. *The Four Winds*, Harper & Row, 1990
Alberto's book is about his early experiences in Peru searching for a 'Hatoon
Laika', a master shaman. This great story takes the reader on many amazing
adventures.

Hyemeyohsts Storm, *Lightningbolt*, Ballantine, 1994
Storm's account of his long apprenticeship with Estcheemah, a Mayan
Zero Chief, who taught him the Medicine Wheel system of knowledge. A
fascinating and multi-levelled work, to be read more than once! Also: *Seven
Arrows*, Ballantine, 1972

Malidoma Some. *Of Water and the Spirit*, Putnam, 1994
The wonderful story of the author's childhood with the Dagara in Burkina
Faso, his capture and indoctrination by the Jesuits, his subsequent 'escape'
and return to his village and the initiation he went through. Enlightening on
many levels. Also: *Ritual Power, Healing and Community*, Gateway Books,
1996

*177*

John Perkins. *The World is as You Dream It*, Destiny Books, 1994
Travels with the Shuar of Equador.

James Hall. *Sangoma*, Touchstone, 1994
An amazing account of the author's apprenticeship in Swaziland to an African tradition.

Richard Katz. *The Straight Path*, Addison Wesley, 1993
The story of two years' studying shamanic healing in Fiji.

Olga Kharitidi. *Entering the Circle*, Thorsons, 1997
A wonderful account of a Russian psychiatrist's initiation into Siberian shamanism.

## Other Related Books

Gabrielle Roth. *Maps to Ecstasy*, New World Library, 1989

Bruce Holbrook. *The Stone Monkey*, William Morrow, 1981

Neil Douglas-Klotz. *Prayers of the Cosmos*, HarperCollins, 1990

Leo Rutherford. *The Book of Games and Warm-ups for Group Leaders*, The Gale Centre / Airlift Books

## Magazines

### UK

*Sacred Hoop*, PO Box 16, Narberth, Pembrokeshire, SA67 8AG. Articles on shamanism and paganism.

*Kindred Spirit*, Foxhole, Dartington, Totnes, Devon TQ9 6EB.

*Caduceus Journal*, 38 Russell Terrace, Leamington Spa, Warwickshire CV31 1HE.

*Resurgence Magazine*, Ford House, Hartland, Bideford, Devon, EX39 6EE.

## USA

*Shaman's Drum*, PO Box 311, Ashland, Oregon 97520.

*Common Boundary*, PO Box 445, Mt Morris, Illinois 61054.

*Magical Blend*, PO Box 600, Chico, California 95927–0600

# *Workshops/Centres*

## *UK*

Eagle's Wing Centre For Contemporary Shamanism, founded by Leo Rutherford, BCM Box 7475, London WC1N 3XX

Sacred Trust, PO Box 603, Bath BA1 2ZU

Faculty of Shamanics, Kenneth and Beryl Meadows, PO Box 300, Potters Bar, Herts EN6 4LE

David Wendl-Berry (vision quest & totem pole therapy), 1 Green Court, Kingstanley, Glos GL10 3QH

Spirit Horse Nomadic Circle, 19 Holmwood Gardens, London N3 3NS

Deer Tribe Lodge of the Singing Stones (Sheffield), tel: 0114 236 8045

Wolf Clan, Anna Gahlin, 7 Eastville, Bath BA1 6QN

Moon Owl Medicine, Heather Campbell, tel: 0141 552 2257

Jonathan Horwitz (shamanic workshops), 29 Chambers Lane, London NW10 2RJ

Shamanic Journeys Training with Jan Wood, tel: 01834 861071. Gatherings with Martine Pretitel, Mayan Shaman. Information: Mark Goodwin, 130 Fulham Road, SW3 6HX

The Moving Centre UK (dance workshops with Ya'Akov and Susannah Darling Khan), Nappers Crossing, Staverton, Devon TQ9 6PD

Caitlin and John Matthews (Celtic shamanism), BCM Hallowquest, London WC1N 3XX

First Fox Medicine (Sharon Forrest), 7 Canal Cottages, Four Crosses, Nr Shrewsbury SY22 6PP

New Life Promotions, Arnica House, 170 Campden Hill Road, London W8 7AS, tel: 0171 938 3788 (Denise Linn and other teachers from abroad)

Monkton Wyld Court, Charmouth, Dorset DT6 6DQ, tel: 01297 560342

Grimstone Manor Community, Yelverton, Devon PL20 7QY, tel: 01822 854358

Earthspirit, Dundon, Somerton, Somerset TA11 6PE, tel: 01458 272161

## USA

Deer Tribe Metis Medicine Society (Harley Swiftdeer), PO Box 12397, Scottsdale, Arizona 85267

The Great Round (vision quests with Sedonia Cahill), PO Box 1076, Forestville, California 95436

Foundation for Shamanic Studies (Michael Harner and Sandra Ingerman), PO Box 1939, Mill Valley, California 94942

Hyemeyohsts Storm, PO Box 11562, Santa Rosa, California 95406

Four Winds Society (Alberto Villoldo), tel: 561 832 9702

Dance Of The Deer Foundation, PO Box 699, Soquel, California 95073

Triquetra Journeys, 26 3rd Street, Brooklyn, New York 11231

## Craft makers

Shamana, Alawn Tickhill, 35 Wilson Avenue, Deal, Kent CT14 9NL